LOST LINES
IRELAND

NIGEL WELBOURN

Ian Allan
PUBLISHING

Contents

First published 2006

ISBN (10) 0 7110 3065 0
ISBN (13) 978 0 7110 3065 7

Published by Ian Allan Publishing

an imprint of Ian Allan Publishing Ltd, Hersham, Surrey KT12 4RG.
Printed in England by Ian Allan Printing Ltd, Hersham, Surrey KT12 4RG.

Code: 0609/B2

Visit the Ian Allan Publishing website at www.ianallanpublishing.com

Key to maps:

———•—— Closed 5ft 3in railway with station or halt

▭▭•▭▭ Closed narrow-gauge railway with station or halt

——— Other railway not subject to chapter text

[Rly] Private or preserved railway or museum

Ⓗ Former railway hotel in use ⌘ closed

Cover photographs courtesy of Colour-Rail

Introduction

Irish railways are unique, in their gauge, character and diversity. They are inextricably linked with Irish history, from the Great Famine to the political upheavals leading to the founding of the Republic. The sometimes turbulent history has involved both murder and mystery.

There were also many parallels with mainland Britain. There has been a continual contraction of the network since its peak in the 1920s, and the need for economies resulted in independent railways being amalgamated into groups. Nationalisation also came to the railways, in Eire under CIE and in Northern Ireland under the UTA. Closures continued, particularly under the UTA.

In addition to the main lines, narrow-gauge lines were built, mostly to serve remote areas. Although constructed to a standard narrow gauge of 3ft, they were both charming and individualistic, and included the first line in the world to run on hydro-electric power and the pioneering use of passenger diesel railcars.

About two thirds of all the railways ever built in Ireland are now closed, including all the narrow-gauge lines. Unwelcome as this has been, it has resulted in Ireland having a substantial number of lost lines. These have put an indelible stamp on the landscape, and even where lines have long been closed, buildings, bridges and many physical remains can still be found. This physical legacy is enriched by some fascinating stories, poems and songs that have survived long after lines have closed. Ireland therefore provides a special appeal to anyone with a nostalgia for lost lines, including the unusual and a whole lost world of rural transport.

The lines in this book, as with others, are loosely ordered geographically from north to south and spellings are in historical context. Irish lines are also included in *Lost Lines: British Narrow Gauge*.

Below: In Ireland it is said that the past is truly a living spirit. A train prepares to leave Listowel on the Lartigue monorail in May 2005, more than 80 years after the original line closed, as the author of this series, seen in the cab, prepares to take you on a journey over Ireland's lost railway lines. *R. Trill*

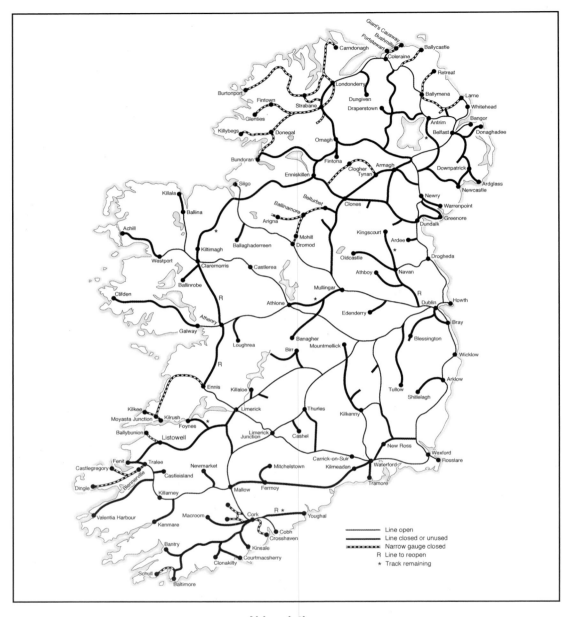

Line open
Line closed or unused
Narrow gauge closed
R Line to reopen
* Track remaining

Abbreviations

BCDR	Belfast & County Down Railway
BNCR	Belfast & Northern Counties Railway
BR	British Railways
CBSCR	Cork, Bandon & South Coast Railway
CDRJC	County Donegal Railways Joint Committee
CLR	Cavan & Leitrim Railway
CIE	Córas Iompair Éireann
GNRB	Great Northern Railway Board
GNR(I)	Great Northern Railway of Ireland
GSR	Great Southern Railways
GSWR	Great Southern & Western Railway
IÉ	Iarnród Éireann
LLSR	Londonderry & Lough Swilly Railway
LMS	London, Midland & Scottish Railway
LNWR	London & North Western Railway
MGWR	Midland Great Western Railway
MR	Midland Railway
NCC	Northern Counties Committee
NIR	Northern Ireland Railways
SLNCR	Sligo, Leitrim & Northern Counties Railway
TDR	Tralee & Dingle Railway
UTA	Ulster Transport Authority

1 Development, division and decline

Early lines

Ireland has limited mineral wealth and, Belfast apart, has never been extensively industrialised, yet a number of mineral tramways existed from early times. A line was operating at Ballycastle in the 1740s, bog railways near Edgeworthstown can be traced back to 1786, and the Arigna Iron Works Tramway opened in 1830.

The first passenger railway in Ireland opened in 1834 and ran south from Dublin to Kingstown (now called Dún Laoghaire); it developed as a commuter route, making a profit and paving the way for other railways. Irish railways were not subsequently built to any sort of national plan, although in more remote areas construction took place under Government subsidy or profit guarantee.

The first main line linked Dublin with Cork in 1849, while the Dublin–Belfast line had opened by 1855. The latter line was built to a 6ft 2in gauge at the Belfast end and 5ft 2in at the Dublin end. Consequently a Gauge Commission was appointed to standardise the gauges in the country. Taking an average between Stephenson's recommendations, of between 5ft and 5ft 6in, it arrived at 5ft 3in, which became the standard gauge throughout Ireland. The narrow-gauge passenger lines in Ireland were usually built to a 3ft gauge, mainly because several early lines had used this gauge. Although cheaper than standard gauge, 3ft was generally considered to be unnecessarily broad, resulting in excessive costs.

Railway construction provided some rural employment during the dark years of the Great Famine of 1845-7, caused by potato blight, but due to emigration the population halved between 1835 and 1935, and this hit railway revenue. William Dargan was the most prominent railway contractor, being responsible for the construction of 800 miles of line. There was little incentive for duplication, although Dublin once had six termini, Cork five, and Londonderry four.

Some significant pre-Grouping companies

The main pre-Grouping companies developed from the amalgamation of smaller companies. The Great Southern & Western Railway opened its ambitious Dublin–Cork main line in 1849 and in 1901 amalgamated with the Waterford, Limerick & Western Railway, becoming the largest of the pre-Grouping companies, with more than 1,000 route miles. A number of its Chief Mechanical Engineers, notably Aspinall, Robinson, H. A. Ivatt and Maunsell, later gained fame on British railways. Its western tentacles from Limerick towards Sligo and Tralee survived into the 1970s.

The Great Northern Railway of Ireland was the second-largest; it linked Dublin with Belfast and also served north-western areas to Bundoran and Londonderry. Trains were smart as well as punctual, and the beautiful sky-blue livery of its engines became legendary. Once a prosperous railway, it was seriously affected by the partition of Ireland, and massive closures of the near-600-mile network ensued.

The Midland Great Western Railway, with more than 500 route miles, covered much of central Ireland,

Below: From the dawn of Irish railways —1846, to be exact — is this Bury, Curtis & Kennedy 2-2-2 with distinctive 'haystack' firebox, hauling two Dublin, Wicklow & Wexford Railway 'toastrack' coaches. This class of locomotive had been taken out of service by 1879, but No 36, posed here by the GSR at Inchicore Works on 18 July 1936, survived and can still be found at Cork station. *Real Photos*

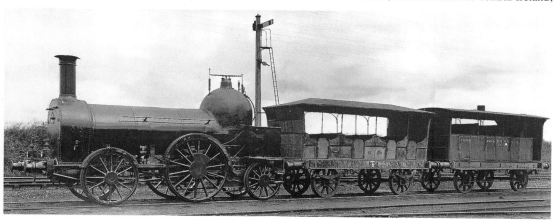

spreading out from Dublin to Galway and Sligo. Its original Dublin terminus at Broadstone was closed in 1937, while western extremities to Killala, Achill and Clifden were also closed in the 1930s.

The Dublin & South Eastern Railway ran from Dublin to Bray, then along the east coast to Wexford and Waterford. Brunel was involved with the construction of the difficult coastal stretch north of Wicklow. The inland Dublin Harcourt Street–Bray line closed in 1958.

A number of smaller railways also developed, one of the most significant being the Belfast & Northern Counties Railway. This became part of Britain's Midland Railway in 1903 and was run by a managing committee based in Belfast, known as the Northern Counties Committee. Three members of the committee were from the Midland Railway, while the other four were Irish members. The main Belfast–Londonderry line was fed by a number of branches to once-prosperous linen towns. The Belfast & County Down Railway covered the area indicated by its title, but only one of its branch lines remains.

The Cork, Bandon & South Coast Railway climbed into the picturesque hills west of Cork to reach Bantry Bay and other rural areas; the Sligo, Leitrim & Northern Counties Railway ran through remote countryside between Enniskillen and Sligo, while the Dundalk, Newry & Greenore Railway was owned by the LNWR. All these lines have been closed completely, and more detailed histories are to be found later in this book.

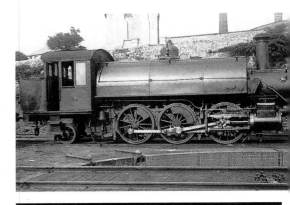

Above: Seen at Cork, on the Cork, Bandon & South Coast Railway, is one of only two American-built 5ft 3in-gauge steam locomotives to work in Ireland. The 0-6-2STs were obtained from Baldwin in 1900 and were of typical US design. Unlike the current American diesel locomotives they proved unsatisfactory and had comparatively short lives, both being scrapped by 1914. *Ian Allan Library*

Below: The remote western end of the MGWR line at Clifden, with MGWR 'K'-class 2-4-0 No 33 *Arrow* on a summer through tourist express to Dublin. The blue and white livery of the coaches was short-lived, as it did not weather well. Note the distinctive 'fly-away' cab, which was later changed to a more conventional design. The Galway–Clifden line would be one of the first major closures, in 1935, but the station house seen here survives, as does that at Recess. *Ian Allan Library*

Narrow gauge

The poverty of much of Ireland provided little incentive for railway construction into remote and thinly populated rural areas, which led to a series of tramway and light-railway Acts, in 1883, 1889 and 1896. These allowed the construction of light railways, which could be built more cheaply than main-line routes and were often narrow-gauge. They enabled the Baronies (later known as county councils) to subsidise lines in remote areas that had no prospect of making a profit.

At their peak there were more than 500 miles of narrow-gauge passenger lines. Although most arrived on the railway scene in the last decades of the 19th century some survived for a remarkably long time, thanks in part to the poor quality of Ireland's roads, and in some cases by making vigorous and innovative economies. For example, in the 1920s the CDRJC was operating railcars and integrating bus services with train timetables.

In 1925 all the lines in Eire were taken over by the Great Southern Railways. Local councils were allowed to phase out their guaranteed payments to light railways over a 10-year period, so from 1935 several lines saw their subsidies disappear, and closures ensued.

Many of the original narrow-gauge lines had effectively been brought into existence by Government funding. Road competition and trans-shipment costs brought about their decline, but ultimately they were also closed by Government, and all had expired by

Above: Ireland led the world in railcar development. No 8, a six-wheeled 74hp Gardner diesel, is seen beside Lough Finn, just outside Fintown, on the CDRJC, on 18 September 1947. The railcar's engine was too wide to allow the wheels to fit directly below, giving an unusual frontal appearance. The railcar had been built as early as 1931 and would be withdrawn in 1949. The narrow-gauge Fintown branch would close to passengers in December 1947 and to all traffic in March 1952. *S. Keyse*

Below: Halcyon narrow-gauge days, when lines ran to many of the remotest areas of Ireland: LLSR 4-8-0 No 12 is seen at Burtonport on 24 June 1937. It was one of a pair of locomotives built in 1905 which were the first in Ireland to have eight-coupled wheels and were the only tender engines to work on the Irish narrow gauge. However, the huge engine became too heavy for the increasingly fragile track, although it was not sold for scrap until 1953. *H. C. Casserley*

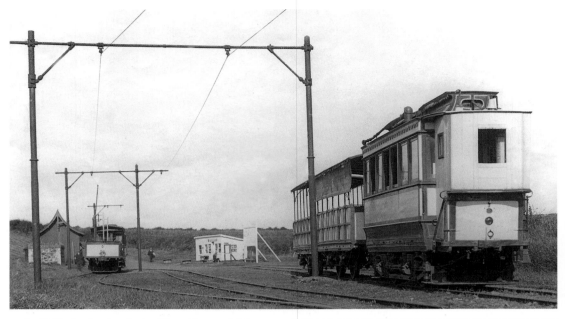

early 1961. In the South the West Clare, which was fully modernised shortly before closure, was the very last to survive, while the last in the North was the CDRJC.

Great Southern Railways and LMS Northern Counties Committee

Turbulent times preceded the amalgamation and division of railways in Ireland. The Easter Rising of 1916 in Dublin led to Pearse, Connolly and others being executed, which in turn fired the momentum towards home rule. The predominantly Protestant north opposed becoming part of the predominantly Catholic Irish Free State, and unrest followed. The conflict spread to the railways, and, by way of example, an attempt was made to derail an Orangemen's special on the Cavan & Leitrim Railway in 1919. The partition of Ireland came in 1922, but discontent with the Anglo-Irish treaty by some in the new Free State led to civil war in 1923/4. Known as 'The Troubles', this resulted in many incidents of damage to railway property, including the destruction of the central arch of a viaduct on the Dublin–Cork main line, a triple collision at Macmine Junction, the burning of more than 40 wagons near Monaghan, and locomotives' being sent careering down the bank at Sligo docks.

Rail mileage peaked in the 1920s at about 3,500 miles, but bus and road competition was already eating into revenue, and in 1925 all railways wholly within the Irish Free State merged to form the Great Southern Railways (GSR). This left a problem for lines in the border area, and partition hastened the demise of the GNR(I), as there were 17 points where this railway crossed the border; this in turn had a detrimental effect

Above: The unique and innovative Giant's Causeway, Portrush & Bush Valley Tramway, with an open electric car on the left and a closed one, with trailer, on the right. This was the first hydro-electric-powered railway in the British Isles, opening in January 1883. The narrow-gauge line ran into financial difficulties after World War 2 and invited the UTA to help; however, this was refused, and the line closed in October 1949. A section has since reopened. *H. C. Casserley*

Above right: Ex-GSWR McDonnell 0-4-4WT No 47 at Castleisland on 13 July 1934, in GSR days. The first of this class of locomotive had appeared in 1869. The Castleisland branch opened in August 1875 and closed to passengers in 1947. Freight for the monthly cattle fairs continued until 1957, when more regular goods trains used the line, continuing until January 1977. The track was lifted in 1988, and today there is no trace of the station. *H. C. Casserley*

Right: The Dundalk, Newry & Greenore Railway's Crewe-built 0-6-0ST No 1 *Macrory* at Newry in November 1951, just before closure of the line. Of unmistakably LNWR design, complete with distinctive chimney and black livery, the locomotive dated from 1876, when the line opened, but was out of use by the time this photograph was taken. It would retain its LNWR livery to the end, ultimately being taken to Dublin for scrapping in 1952. *BR*

on passenger convenience and long-established freight routes.

In Northern Ireland, in 1923 the Northern Counties Committee formally became part of the London, Midland & Scottish Railway (LMS). Considerable improvements were made by the LMS, resulting in the Belfast–Londonderry and Belfast–Larne lines' becoming the most modern in Ireland, while the LMS's crimson-lake livery was adopted for coaches and locomotives.

In 1933 there was a 12-week strike by many railway staff in Ireland. In the same year the LMS made

economies, including allowing the GNR(I) to take over the former Dundalk, Newry & Greenore Railway. In the South the GSR was also forced to make economies, closing the Kinsale, Clifden and Achill branches in the 1930s. The coal shortages associated with World War 2, known in Eire as 'The Emergency', resulted in branch lines' closing for long periods, while the severe winter of 1947 was to cause similar problems.

Ulster Transport Authority

In 1948 LMS interests in Northern Ireland became part of the nationalised British Railways, while the 1948 Transport Act (Northern Ireland) established the UTA; this new Government-run organisation took over the former NCC lines and the Belfast & County Down Railway in October 1948. In 1953 the Great Northern Railway Board was established to run the loss-making former GNR(I), but in 1958 the railway was divided between the northern and southern governments, the UTA getting its hands on all the former GNR(I) lines in the north. The UTA had an overwhelmingly anti-railway policy from its inception and became known as Ulster's Track Abandoners. Ignoring opposition, it closed almost all of the BCDR and ex-GNR(I) main lines north of the border, leaving CIE with no real choice but to follow suit. The drastic UTA closures, involving more than 450 miles of line, particularly in the border areas, left a gaping hole in the railway map of Ireland.

Steam continued, but the UTA painted its engines — including many of the beautiful sky-blue

locomotives inherited from the GNR(I) — black, while its passenger stock was a drab dark green. In April 1968 the UTA's remaining railway assets were handed over to Northern Ireland Railways.

Córas Iompair Éireann

In the Republic the Irish Transport Company, Córas Iompair Éireann, began operating in January 1945, merging the Great Southern Railways with Dublin Transport. Full nationalisation came in 1950. In its early years the Republic's economy was not very strong, and the new organisation was starved of resources. Gas-lit clerestory coaches were still used on express trains in 1956, and six-wheeled wooden stock on the Youghal line in 1957. In October 1958 the GNRB in Eire was also absorbed by CIE.

Modernisation did come eventually, and CIE was 'dieselised' early on, mainly because Irish steam coal was not available and the fuel crisis of 1947 had crippled the system. After 1963 no regular steam workings remained, and Eire was the first country in Europe to be completely dieselised. Although CIE resisted the extensive cuts seen in the North a number of closures were agreed in the 1960s, including the Cork–Bantry line and the Valencia Harbour route. By the 1970s the run-down suburban system in Dublin could have been abandoned, and in the early 1980s further retrenchment measures were announced, but in 1987 the railways in Eire became a separate CIE division known as Iarnród Éireann, or Irish Rail. The 1990s saw the economy of Eire revitalised, and with it came increased investment in the railways.

Left: The Cookstown branch was one casualty in a spate of UTA closures. Seen at Cookstown on 12 June 1954 is ex-GNR(I) 'SG2' 0-6-0 No 19 with a train from Dungannon. The NCC also operated a branch to Cookstown, and the two stations adjoined one another. The ex-NCC branch would close to passengers in 1950 and to freight in 1955, the ex-GNR(I) line closing to passengers in 1956 and to freight three years later. A section of the branch from Dungannon to Coalisland was to survive as a coal siding until 1965. *A. Porter*

Above right: Eire became the first country in Europe to be fully 'dieselised' — steam working was drastically reduced in the early 1960s, and regular workings ended in 1963. Built by General Motors in 1960, No B128 is seen here at Tuam with a train from Galway on 1 April 1963. Tuam would close in 1976, but rusting tracks remain. The station may reopen under plans for a revival of the Western Rail Corridor. The '121'-class diesels ended service in 2005, although No B128 was scrapped a little earlier. *R. Joanes*

Centre right: Demolition work in progress at Fairytown Bridge, between Clonsilla and Navan, on 16 July 1964. The line was single at this point, but a long siding was provided here. The demolition train used on this route was powered by ex-GNR(I) railcar A, latterly UTA No 101, the single line being lifted at the rate of about half a mile a day. Plans for a phased reopening are in prospect. *E. Patterson*

Right: Built in 1858, Foynes station closed to passengers in February 1963. The main stone-built station structure remained in good condition, but by May 2005, when this photograph was taken, the overall roof was in a poor state of repair. The Limerick–Foynes line has remained 'mothballed', pending the possible reintroduction of a freight service, since its closure to freight in December 2001. *Author*

2 A geographical perspective

Railway construction in Ireland was not constrained by overwhelming physical problems, and there are few significant tunnels or bridges, the Boyne Bridge being the greatest civil-engineering work. However, there were many watercourses to cross, and some sections of line proved difficult and expensive to construct. Nevertheless, all the main towns of Ireland at one time had rail access.

Geographically, the mountains of Ireland are broadly found around the coast. In Donegal the confines of the Barnes Gap were used by the LLSR to reach the Atlantic coast, while the gap at Barnesmore was used by the CDRJC. The Antrim Plateau basalt, which at the Giant's Causeway splits to form hexagonal columns, provided the railways with a spectacular tourist attraction. Near Retreat the narrow-gauge Ballymena–Retreat line reached 1,045ft, the highest point on any Irish passenger railway. The southern mountains include those in Kerry, where the steeply graded TDR crossed the Slieve Mish range. Between the mountain ranges is to be found the central and sometimes boggy plain through which flows Ireland's longest river, the Shannon.

Ireland was mainly rural, with little heavy industry outside Belfast, but Anglo-Irish trade led to the development of a number of railway-operated packet

Below: Map of Ireland's railways in 1906: note the high concentration of stations at Cork and Belfast. *Author's collection*

Above right: A Great Western Railway enamelled poster highlighting the 'new' Fishguard route from Paddington to southern Ireland. Fishguard replaced Neyland as the GWR's main packet port for Ireland in 1906, giving a clue as to the date of the poster. *Author's collection*

Centre right: Ireland's many watercourses had to be crossed by the railways. Weir's Bridge, the 467ft-long girder bridge over the narrows of the River Erne (and also known as Killyhevlin Viaduct), was located 1 mile west of Enniskillen station and was the major civil-engineering work on the SLNCR. A 5mph speed restriction was imposed on the bridge, which is seen here on 22 December 1955. The line would close to all traffic in October 1957. *C. Matherson*

Lower right: The disused 91yd Drung Hill No 2 Tunnel on the Farranfore–Valentia Harbour line, seen in May 2005; a short gap separated this tunnel from the longer Drung Hill No 1 Tunnel. The line ran between the Teermoyle Mountains and Dingle Bay, and nearby a 50yd stone roof protected the track from rock falls in this area. *Author*

Far right: The remains of the Corrib Viaduct at Galway give an indication of how substantially some of the Baronial lines were built. The viaduct had three 150ft spans and a 21ft bascule opening section. Built in 1895, it ceased to be used in 1935. The metal sections have long since been removed, but the substantial stone piers remain in the River Corrib and are seen here in August 2005. *Author*

ports, so called because they dealt with mail packets. For passenger convenience they were generally located on the shortest sea crossings to Ireland. Larne–Stranraer provided the shortest main route, but Holyhead–Dublin developed as the most important and was served by the first-ever named train, the 'Irish Mail' from London. The Fishguard–Rosslare ferries developed as the main crossing for the south, but several other ferry links were also established. A number of far-flung, wild and remote harbours were once also served by rail, and the export of live cattle was important. Valentia Harbour was the most westerly railway point in Europe.

Geologically, an absence of extensive mineral ores, together with thin deposits of poor-grade coal, stifled industrialisation, although shipbuilding was once important at Belfast. Bauxite and copper were found, and zinc was still being conveyed by rail in 2006. Peat is also extracted and still supports an extensive network of narrow-gauge lines.

Climatically, mild winters and rain-bearing westerly winds created ideal conditions for livestock. Railways opened up remote agricultural areas, and cattle became the main freight on many lines. In exposed western parts gales could derail narrow-gauge trains, and at Owencarrow Viaduct, on the Londonderry & Lough Swilly Railway, in 1925 four passengers were killed; following this incident an anemometer installed on the line recorded winds of up to 112mph.

Politically, the partition of Ireland had a considerable effect on the railways, particularly in the border areas. Today just one railway line crosses the border between Northern Ireland and the Republic.

③ The killing of the County Down

The Belfast & County Down Railway ran from its Belfast terminus at Queen's Quay into County Down. It absorbed a number of local lines and enjoyed a virtual monopoly in the area, serving the county town of Downpatrick, together with a number of fishing ports and market towns. The first section of what was to become the main line opened from Belfast to Comber in May 1850 and was extended southward to Ballynahinch by September 1858. This in turn became the end of a 3½-mile branch from Ballynahinch Junction when the main line was extended further south to Downpatrick and thence to Newcastle by March 1869.

The Comber–Donaghadee branch had opened in June 1861, but a link to the harbour at Donaghadee was not opened until March 1870. It was intended that this new harbour should act as an important ferry route to Portpatrick in Scotland, but services lasted for only two years, the Larne–Stranraer route proving more popular.

The Downpatrick–Ardglass branch opened in May 1892, while in September of that year a new spur at Downpatrick allowed Belfast–Newcastle trains to run through without reversing.

Newcastle developed as a fashionable seaside and golfing resort 'where the Mountains of Mourne sweep

Below: The imposing, spacious, light and airy interior of the extended Belfast Queen's Quay station c1920, with a train of both six-wheeled and bogie stock at No 3 platform. In the foreground is the BCDR Royal Saloon, No 153, which still survives at the Downpatrick Railway Museum. Military personnel are noted on the new No 1 platform. *Ian Allan Library*

down to the sea', and 1898 saw the opening of the impressive Slieve Donard Hotel. A Newcastle–Castlewellan link to join the GNR(I) line from Scarva was eventually opened in March 1906, providing a gateway for tourists from other parts of Ireland, and a new station at Newcastle, close to the shoreline, opened in the same year.

At its peak the railway operated about 80 route miles of (mainly single) line, 30 locomotives, 180 carriages and more than 700 wagons. Between 1910 and 1914 the BCDR terminus station at Belfast Queen's Quay was rebuilt and extended to five platforms to cope with growing passenger traffic; a covered area was served by Belfast trams until 1954.

In 1948 the UTA took over and, with its anti-rail stance, wasted no time in reducing the timetable and killing the railway. The Comber–Downpatrick–Newcastle lines, together with the Ardglass branch, were closed to all traffic in January 1950, the remaining Ballymacarrett Junction–Comber–Donaghadee line, which conveyed many commuters to Belfast, succumbing in April of the same year. The attractive Beyer Peacock 4-4-2Ts and the 4-6-4Ts were all scrapped by 1956, save for one 4-4-2T that survived into preservation.

The Newcastle–Castlewellan section was operated jointly with the GNRB, which was reluctant to close it. The UTA withdrew its trains in April 1950, but the line continued to be used by GNRB trains until closure in May 1955. Thereafter the station at Newcastle lay derelict, with track becoming overgrown, for a while after closure, as if in disbelief at the fate of the once-proud BCDR.

The Downpatrick Railway Museum has reopened a section of the ex-BCDR line at Downpatrick, while at Newcastle the ex-BCDR Slieve Donard Hotel and much of the station building, including the clock tower, also survive. Lesser remains of the BCDR can still be found throughout County Down. Trains on the ex-BCDR Bangor branch continued to use Belfast Queen's Quay until the station was closed by NIR in April 1976. They now run into Belfast Central, allowing connections to other parts of the rail network that were never available from the original BCDR terminus.

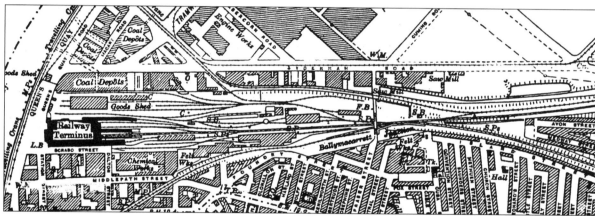

Above: Map of the BCDR's Queen's Quay station in 1938. *Crown copyright*

Right: Ex-BCDR Beyer Peacock-built 4-4-2T No 17 stands in the station at Belfast Queen's Quay on 6 September 1949, possibly on a 'Bangor and back for a bob' train. The locomotive would be scrapped in 1956, Queen's Quay station closing 20 years later. *I. Cochrane*

Above: Harland & Wolff-built 270hp diesel-electric locomotive No D1 is seen just outside Ballymacarrett shed at Belfast on 29 July 1944. The signal gantry was the largest in Ireland. Harland & Wolff tried to break into the railway-diesel market when shipping orders were low, supplying this engine to the BCDR in 1933. It would later be used on Harland & Wolff's own dockside lines, with centre wheels removed to provide greater flexibility on the sharp curves. *Ian Allan Library*

Centre left: To differentiate it from ex-NCC stock ex-BCDR 4-4-2T No 19 had 200 added to its number by the UTA, being seen here as No 219 at Donaghadee station on 23 April 1950. At one time coaches were 'slipped' for the branch from Comber to Donaghadee, a seaside town whose aspirations to become a packet port were never realised; the branch closed on the day this photograph was taken. *E. Patterson*

Lower left: Downpatrick station was located close to Down Cathedral. The terminus acted as the junction for the branch to Ardglass, while a spur line enabled Belfast–Newcastle trains to run direct, avoiding reversal. The station and overall roof, seen here in the 1930s, would be demolished after closure, although the area is now used by the Downpatrick Railway Museum. *Ian Allan Library*

Above: Newcastle station in the 1930s, with GNR(I) 'P'-class 4-4-0 No 89 at the platform and the distinctive station clock tower in the background. Newcastle was an attractive resort, and the station, used by BCDR and GNR(I) services, was well placed for the town and the sea. In 1907 four porters were employed, and an exclusive footpath link ran from the station to the railway-owned hotel. *Ian Allan Library*

Right: Map of railways in the Downpatrick area in 1902. *Crown copyright*

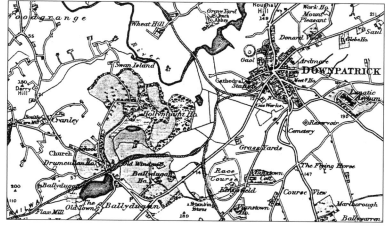

Right: Belfast suffered much bomb damage during World War 2 and Queen's Quay station was hit in 1941. However, the protective canopy on the front of the station and the attractive mouldings were crudely ripped away by the UTA. Consequently in the 1960s the station looked shabby and neglected, while bus passengers had to wait in the open. The station would be demolished after closure in 1976. *Hugh Davis*

Above: End of the line. The clock tower at Newcastle station, rebuilt in 1906, represented the southern extremity of the BCDR. The huge porte-cochère that once graced the front of the distinctively designed station reached almost to the clock face itself, but after closure in 1955 this, together with the platforms, was demolished. However, the main red-brick station building and clock tower remain, and the clock was still indicating the right time when this view was recorded in August 2003. Author

Left: Tullymurry new station, as seen in August 2003. The buildings date from 1896, when they replaced the original station of 1871, and are built to a standard BCDR design in Belfast red brick with blue brick dressings. Located in a remote rural area, the station became a centre for agricultural produce. The station house survives as a private residence. Author

4 Steaming at Belfast

By 1900 Belfast was the third-busiest port in the British Isles, and this, together with shipbuilding and linen production, provided much traffic for the railways. At that time the main railways serving Belfast all had their own termini. The BCDR station was at Queen's Quay, the GNR(I) at Great Victoria Street, and the BNCR at York Road. The Belfast Central Railway, which became part of the GNR(I) in 1885, provided a link to the BCDR. In addition the BNCR could be reached from the other railways by means of various freight lines.

The railways also all had their own steam depots in the city. The BNCR shed was outside York Road station, and the BCDR shed was just outside Queen's Quay station at Ballymacarrett. In 1911 the largest shed in Northern Ireland, which could house more than 55 locomotives and included a reversing triangle, was that opened by the GNR(I) at Adelaide, to the south of the city.

During World War 2 death and destruction was inflicted on Belfast, including damage to stations, York Road in particular. Nevertheless, the Ulster Transport Authority, established postwar, managed to destroy much more of Ulster's railway network. Indeed, such was the UTA's anti-rail bias that it even considered proposals to single the Belfast–Dublin main line. Yet its policy was to see steam remain long after it ended in the south, and good use was made elsewhere in the North of the relatively modern 2-6-4Ts, as an alternative to investing in new diesel locomotives.

Right: Smartly turned-out Beyer Peacock 4-4-2T No 16 is seen on 17 March 1948 near Ballymacarrett shed, which was located just outside Belfast Queen's Quay station. At one time the BCDR allocated two dedicated sets of crews to each of its locomotives, a practice that did much to keep the locomotives in good order, as apparent from this view.
H. C. Casserley

Right: Increasing patronage on the BCDR in the 1920s required more powerful locomotives. Huge Baltic (4-6-4) tank No 24, weighing more than 80 tons, is seen in filthy condition at Ballymacarrett on 31 July 1949. Although of a modern design these locomotives were not superheated and were surprisingly sluggish; they were also heavy on coal, being sometimes nicknamed 'the miner's friends'. *M. Livesey*

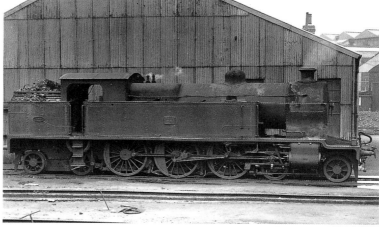

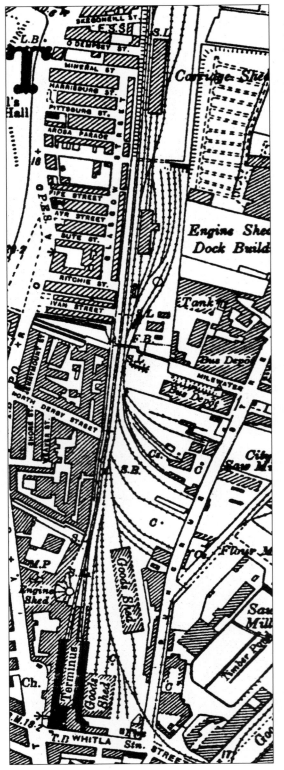

Queen's Quay shed was the first to close, in 1954, although derelict ex-BCDR engines remained present until 1956. Adelaide shed closed in November 1966, and the buildings were demolished. By 1967 only eight steam locomotives remained in use in the North, and 1971 saw the last example cease normal work. York Road was thus the last main-line steam shed in the whole of the UK to close.

Further upheaval, albeit of a generally more positive nature, was to follow after the UTA had been replaced by NIR. Belfast Queen's Quay station was closed in April 1976, together with Great Victoria Street, to make way for the new Belfast Central station, which opened at the same time on the site of the former Maysfields cattle yard. Nevertheless, the Belfast Central Junction–Great Victoria Street line closed at the same time, the ex-GNR(I) station subsequently being demolished.

York Road station closed in 1992 and was replaced by a new station, Yorkgate. This became a through station two years later, when a new 1¾-mile cross-harbour link was provided to Belfast Central; a maintenance depot was built on part of the site of the old York Road station. The new Belfast Central station was a little way from the city centre, and consequently a new Great Victoria Street station, closer to the heart of the city, opened in September 1995.

Left: Map of Belfast York Road shed in 1938. *Crown copyright*

Above right: Pictured at Belfast York Road, No 50 *Jubilee* was built as a 2-4-0 compound for the BNCR by Beyer, Peacock & Co in 1895, being rebuilt as a 4-4-0 two years later and as a simple in 1926. The massive (7ft) driving wheels were the largest ever used in Ireland. Pictured in 1937, the locomotive would be withdrawn in 1946. *H. C. Casserley*

Centre right: NCC 0-6-0T No 18 was one of two standard LMS 'Jinties' that were re-gauged and transferred to Ireland in 1944, to alleviate wartime pressures on the NCC lines. Formerly LMS No 7456, it is seen in faded NCC livery at Belfast on 17 April 1948. *H. C. Casserley*

Right: Belfast Harbour on 24 August 1964, with ex-SLNCR 0-6-4T *Lough Melvin* and a flag-waving guard. One of the last two conventional steam engines delivered to Ireland, in 1951, the locomotive had been transferred to the UTA upon closure of the SLNCR and would be withdrawn in 1965. At one time the Belfast Harbour lines were some 16 miles in length and were very busy with freight traffic. *Ian Allan Library*

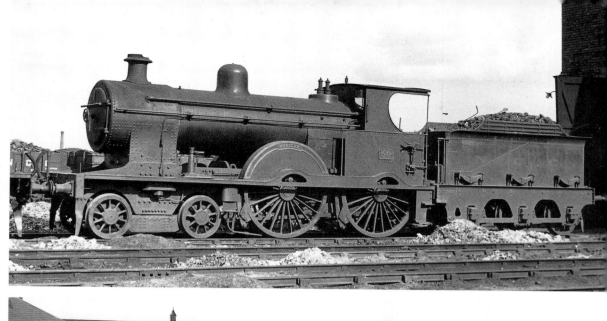

Left: Adelaide shed in 1959, with Class PPs 4-4-0 No 74X, an ex-GNR(I) locomotive formerly named *Rostrevor*. James Park came from the GNR in England to join the GNR(I) and was responsible for the design, the Doncaster influence being apparent in the chimney and cab. The 'X' number suffix added in later years by the UTA indicated that a locomotive was scheduled for withdrawal as soon as heavy repairs became necessary. *D. Anderson*

Left: GNR(I) Class V 4-4-0 No 86 *Peregrine* simmers in its sky-blue livery at Belfast Adelaide shed on 30 August 1958; even the UTA drew back from repainting these beautiful compound locomotives in its drab black. This engine would be scrapped a few years later, but fortunately one of the class has been preserved. *D. Anderson*

Below: Ex-GNR(I) 4-4-0 No 207 *Boyne* in its splendid sky-blue livery at Adelaide shed in April 1965. The 66¼-ton engine, built in 1948, was one of the last main-line locomotives built for the GNR(I). These were also the last 4-4-0 express locomotives in the UK and the only Irish locomotives with smoke-deflectors. None of the class would survive the scrapman's torch, but clearly steam in Ireland was lovely while it lasted. *M. Pope*

Right: Adelaide shed again, this time on 10 July 1964. On the left is UTA No 47, an ex-GNR(I) Class UG 0-6-0 dating from 1937 and destined to be scrapped in 1965; on the right is ex-NCC Class WT 'Jeep' 2-6-4T No 57, the last of a batch of mixed-traffic locomotives built at Derby in 1949. So nicknamed because of their versatility, the 'Jeeps' would survive into the NIR era, ultimately being scrapped by the early 1970s, with the exception of No 4, preserved by the RPSI.
W. Sumner

Centre right: A general view of York Road shed on 23 August 1969, with the concrete mechanical coaling plant, erected by the NCC in the 1930s and sometimes known as 'The Cenotaph', dominating the scene. This was one of just three such plants in the whole of Ireland. Locomotives on shed include Class WT 2-6-4Ts Nos 4, 5, 50, 51, 53, 55 and an ex-SLNCR engine, UTA No 27, of which Nos 4 and 27 would be saved from scrap by the Railway Preservation Society of Ireland. *D. Idle*

Below right: Ex-GNR(I) 4-4-0 No 171 *Slieve Gullion* photographed at Harland & Wolff's yard in May 1968 against a background of heavy industrial plant once associated with shipbuilding at Belfast, including the construction of the *Titanic*. The locomotive was another to be preserved by the RPSI.
W. Boomer

Above: Adelaide shed was demolished after closure in 1966, and today none of the original locoshed buildings remains. The site still sees some rail training and other uses, although the freight depot opened on the site by NIR in 1972 was out of use when this photograph was taken in August 2005. *Author*

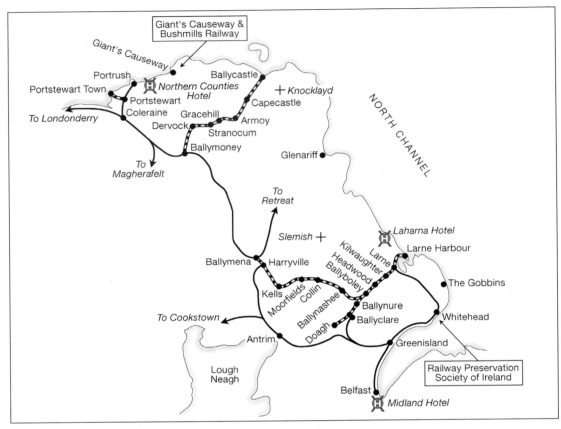

Boat train to Ballymena

The Larne Harbour–Ballyclare section of the narrow-gauge (3ft) Ballymena & Larne Railway opened in August 1877 for iron-ore traffic, the entire line to Ballymena opening to all traffic a year later. The Ballyclare–Doagh extension opened to all traffic in May 1884, increasing the route network to 31 miles. The railway became part of the BNCR in 1899 and the NCC in 1903. Somersault signals and locomotives painted a convincing 'Midland' red gave the line a particularly English atmosphere, and the route became part of the LMS in 1923, when that railway assumed control of the NCC. On this line ran the Larne–Ballymena boat train, the only truly narrow-gauge express in Ireland, which covered the 25¼-mile route in an hour. Three new coaches were provided for the service in 1928.

Freight was also important. On one occasion a freight train appeared to be missing a wagon on arrival at Larne, but as nothing seemed amiss it was at first assumed that it was a simple counting error. However, later the wagon was found at the bottom of an embankment at Ballynashee, which means 'the place of the fairies'. How the wagon found its way there and how its cargo of Irish whiskey became lost remains a mystery. Some blamed the banshee …

Passenger services on the Doagh branch ended in October 1930, while the main Larne–Ballymena section closed to passengers in February 1933, bringing to an end the famous boat trains. The Ballymena–Ballyboley Junction section closed to remaining freight in June 1940, the Ballyclare–Doagh section following two years later.

After passenger closure the boat-train coaches were transferred to the Ballycastle line, and when that railway closed the stock ended up on the CDRJC. As soon as the UTA took over in 1948 the prospects looked bleak; maintenance was cut back, and the remaining freight section between Larne Harbour and Ballyclare paper mill closed in July 1950.

24

Above: A view of Larne Town c1890, with Beyer Peacock 2-4-0T No 64, built in 1878. Of a general type still to be found on the Isle of Man, the locomotive would be sold to the Castlederg & Victoria Bridge Tramway in 1928 and scrapped when that line closed in 1933. *LPC*

Right: NCC No 113, a 4-4-2T Kitson-built engine of 1908, between Larne Harbour and Larne Town on 22 June 1937. Originally from the steeply graded Ballycastle Railway, this type was found to be rather heavy and slipped badly on that line's gradients. Consequently they were transferred to the Larne line, where boiler mountings had to be cut down to fit the loading gauge. By this time the Larne line was freight-only but was some way off being closed by the UTA. The (Irish) standard-gauge Larne–Belfast line is on the right. *H. C. Casserley*

Below: Larne–Doagh–Ballymena timetable, April 1910.

LARNE, DOAGH, and BALLYMENA (Narrow Gauge Branch).—Midland (Northern Counties of Ireland).

Down. — Week Days.

Miles	Down.	mrn	mrn	mrn	mrn	mrn	aft	aft
	Larne Harbour dep.	....	7 51	Saturdays only.	....	....	2 15	....
1	Larne	6 35	....		8 40	1015	2 20	6 55
6½	Headwood	Sig.	....		Sig.	Sig.	Sig.	Sig.
7¾	Ballyboley	7 0	....		9 5	1045	2 40	7 20
—	Ballyboley dep.	7 10	....		9 10	1055	2 45	7 25
9½	Ballynure	7 15	....		9 18	11 3	2 53	7 33
11½	Ballyclare 927	7 20	....		9 26	1111	3 0	7 41
13½	Doagh arr.	7 30	....		9 35	1120	3 10	7 50
—	Mls Doagh dep.	6 35	....	8 0	Stops at Kilwaughter.	1025	2 10	6 25
—	2 Ballyclare 927	6 43	....	8 5		1033	2 18	6 40
—	4 Ballynure	6 50	....	8 10		1040	2 25	6 50
—	5¾ Ballyboley arr.	6 55	....	8 15		1045	2 33	7 0
12	Ballynashee	7 25	....	8 35		1115	3 0	7 40
—	Collin	7c27	....	Sig.		Sig.	Sig.	Sig.
17½	Moorfields	7 40	....	8 50		1133	3 13	7 55
20½	Kells	7 48	a	8 58		1143	3 23	8 5
25¼	Ballymena 927 arr.	8 5	8 51	9 10		12 5	3 35	8 25

Fourth mrn train: Runs on 3rd Wednesday and Ballyclare Half-yearly Fair Days. 2 15 aft train: Runs 20 minutes later on Sats.

Up. — Week Days.

Miles	Up.	mrn	mrn	mrn	aft	aft	aft
	Ballymena dep.	6d15	Stops at Kilwaughter.	10 0	1 40	5 50	6 15
4¾	Kells	6 30		1015	2 0	....	6 37
7¾	Moorfields	6 40		1023	2 8	....	6 45
—	Collin	6h45		Sig.	Sig.	....	Sig.
13¼	Ballynashee	6 57		1035	2 25	....	7 2
17¼	Ballyboley	7 10		1045	2 38	....	7 15
—	Ballyboley dep.	7 10		1055	2 45	....	7 25
19¼	Ballynure	7 15		11 3	2 53	....	7 33
20¾	Ballyclare 927	7 20		1111	3 0	....	7 41
23¼	Doagh arr.	7 30		1120	3 10	....	7 50
—	Mls Doagh dep.	6 35	8 0	1025	2 10	....	6 25
—	2 Ballyclare 927	6 43	8 8	1033	2 18	....	6 40
—	4 Ballynure	6 50	8 15	1040	2 25	....	6 50
—	5¾ Ballyboley arr.	6 55	8 20	1045	2 33	....	7 0
19	Headwood	Sig.	Sig.	Sig.	Sig.	....	Sig.
24½	Larne 929	7 45	8 50	1110	3 5	....	7 45
25¼	Larne Harbour arr.	....	....	1115	3 15	6 50	7 50

Second mrn train: Runs on 2nd Thursday and Larne Half-yearly Fair Days. 1 40 aft train: Runs 20 minutes later on Sats.

a Stops at Kells, except on Sats. *c* Stops on Ballymena Market and Fair Days. *d* Starts from **Harryville** Station. *h* Stops on Larne Market and Fair Days.

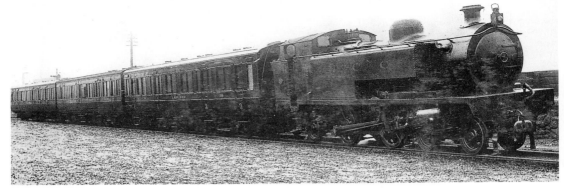

Above: An ex-Ballycastle Railway 4-4-2T, by now NCC No 113, poses with the three coaches of the Larne boat train at Larne Harbour. This train represented the height of luxury for Irish narrow-gauge: the coaches were massive, at 52ft in length and 7ft 10in wide, and had corridor connections, electric lights, steam heating and toilets. The Larne crossing was the setting for Sir John Magill's Last Journey, a mystery detective story based on the NCC. *LPC*

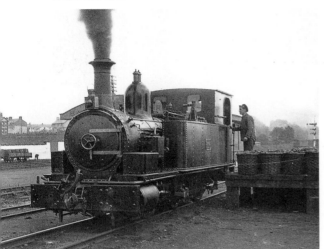

Left: Locomotives were exchanged between the NCC's narrow-gauge lines; here No 106, an ex-Ballymena & Larne 0-6-0T, takes on coal at Ballymoney in 1931. Built by Beyer Peacock in 1883, it is in its final form with Ross 'Pop' safety valves on the boiler dome. It would be withdrawn in 1933. *Ian Allan Library*

Below: NCC No 41, a 2-4-2T compound built by Beyer Peacock in 1909, shunts at Ballycastle station in the 1940s. At one time the NCC livery was known as 'invisible green', but it was later changed to the striking Midland red. This locomotive would survive to be repainted in UTA lined black with new insignia but would nevertheless be scrapped in 1954. *E. Patterson*

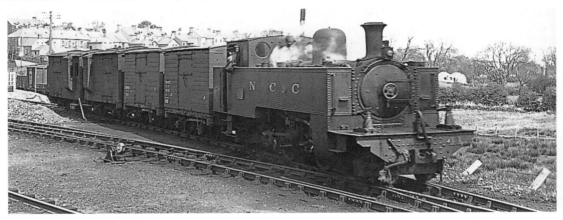

BALLYCASTLE and BALLYMONEY.—Ballycastle.

Sec. and Gen. Man., H. M'Allen, Ballymoney.

Miles	Up.	Week Days.					Sn	Miles	Down.	Week Days.						Sn
		mrn	mrn	aft	aft	aft	aft		York Road,	mrn	mrn	mrn	non	aft	aft	aft	mrn
	Ballycastle....dep.	6 50	1030	2 15	4 10	6 25	3 30		926 Belfast...dep.	6 30	8 0	9 45	12 0			12 25	7 0
3¼	Capecastle	7 0	1040	2 26	4 20	6 35	3 40	—	Ballymoney...dep.	8 20	1015	1 0	1 20	1 40		2 30	9 5
6	Armoy	7 8	1052	2 37	4 28	6 45	3 48	4½	Dervock	8 34	1029	1 17		1 57		2 47	9 19
8¼	Gracehill.........	Th.	Th.					6½	Stranocum	8 41	1036	1 26		2 6		2 56	9 26
9¼	Stranocum	7 18	11 4	2 49	4 38	6 55	3 58	8	Gracehill.........		Th.			Sig.			
11¼	Dervock........[927	7 25	1113	2 58	4 45	7 5	4 5	10½	Armoy	8 52	1050	1 38		2 18		3 8	9 37
16¼	Ballymoney 926, arr.	7 40	1130	3 15	5 0	7 20	4 20	13	Capecastle	9 1	1058	1 49		2 29		3 19	9 46
69¼	927 Belfast†....arr.	9 45	2 40	6 0	6 50	10 6	35	16½	Ballycastle ...arr.	9 10	11 7	2 0	2 0	2 40		3 30	6 10 9 55

Runs on the 12th instant only.
Except Sats.
Sats. only.
Sats. only.
Thursdays only.

† York Road Station.

Right: Ballycastle station in UTA days, with two 2-4-2T compounds, including No 41, waiting to depart on 20 May 1950. The coaches are from the Larne boat train and in later years had their corridor connections blocked off. Ballycastle station once had four NCC camping coaches, while special trains were run in connection with summer events.
H. C. Casserley

The Ballycastle Railway

Opened in October 1880, the narrow-gauge (3ft) Ballycastle Railway ran some 16¼ miles from Ballymoney, on the main Belfast–Londonderry line, to the coastal town of Ballycastle, just 15 miles from Scotland. The coastal end of the line required both a tunnel and a viaduct in order to reach the terminus. A proposed branch from Dervock to Bushmills was never built. The line remained independent but went bankrupt in 1924, all services being suspended in April of that year. However, it was taken over by the NCC and reopened in August.

Ballycastle continued to develop as a coastal resort, and extra trains were run in the holiday season — even the Larne boat-train stock was transferred to the line to cope with holiday traffic. Something of a mystery in itself lay in the fact that, having overhauled and repainted one of the locomotives following takeover, the UTA promptly agreed that the line be made a priority for closure. All services ceased in July 1950, and the line was dismantled a few years later.

Below left: Ballycastle–Ballymoney timetable, April 1910.

Right: UTA closure notice, 1950.

WITHDRAWAL OF RAILWAY SERVICES

BETWEEN BALLYMONEY AND BALLYCASTLE

On and from MONDAY, the 3rd of JULY, 1950, the Section of the Authority's Narrow Gauge Railway Line between Ballymoney and Ballycastle will be closed to all passenger and goods traffic, and Railway Services will no longer be available at the following Stations and Halts:

DERVOCK	ARMOY
STRANOCUM	CAPECASTLE
GRACEHILL	BALLYCASTLE

Time Tables of Augmented Road Passenger Services

Road Services will replace the Railway Services to be withdrawn. Time Tables of the Road Passenger Services are shown on Pages 284-285 and 346-348 of the large combined Time Table, and on Pages 110-111, 140-142 of sectional Time Table No. 5, dated 19th June, 1950.

A Leaflet Time Table will also be available to the public on Friday, 23rd June, 1950, and may be obtained on application at local offices and depots of the Authority.

Issue of Railway Tickets

Rail fares between Ballymoney and Ballycastle and intermediate halts will be cancelled and bus fares will apply.

The issue of ordinary railway tickets from Ballycastle to stations beyond Ballymoney (including Cross-channel stations) will be continued. Passengers must obtain such tickets at Ballycastle station before boarding omnibuses.

Similarly, through ordinary railway tickets will continue to be issued to Ballycastle from the Northern Counties stations and Cross-channel stations.

These tickets will be valid by connecting omnibuses from Ballycastle to Ballymoney and vice versa. In addition, tickets issued to stations south of Ballymena will be available by connecting omnibuses from Ballycastle to Ballymena and vice versa.

Unexpired Railway Tickets

Passengers holding unexpired railway tickets may travel by bus without extra charge during the period of their validity. If the holders wish to surrender such tickets appropriate refunds will be made.

Parcels by Passenger Services

Parcels will be accepted for conveyance by the Authority's services at Ballycastle station as heretofore. Parcels not exceeding 56 lbs. will be accepted at Stranocum and Armoy by the Parcels Agents enumerated below for conveyance by omnibus services.

The Authority's representation in the area will be as follows:

Mr. J. M'Callion, District Traffic Manager, Ulster Transport Authority, The Railway Station, Coleraine. Phone, Coleraine 466.

BALLYMONEY STATION—Phone, Ballymoney 5.

STRANOCUM—Miss A. Cross, Grocer, Stranocum (Bus Parcels only).

ARMOY—Mr. C. Malloy, Grocer, Armoy (Bus Parcels only); F. & A. Cusick, Post Office, Armoy (Phone, Armoy 200); Freight.

BALLYCASTLE STATION—Phone, Ballycastle 365.

The Authority are confident that the Transport requirements of the Public will be fully met by the new arrangements, but if any further information is desired, the public are invited to communicate with the above, or with Mr. R. E. M. Hughes, Passenger Manager, or Mr. H. C. Botshi, Acting Freight Manager, Headquarters, 21 Linenhall Street, Belfast.

ULSTER TRANSPORT AUTHORITY
22nd June, 1950.

The Portstewart Tramway

The Portstewart Tramway opened in June 1882 as the first roadside steam tramway in Ireland. The narrow-gauge (3ft) single line ran for 1¾ miles along the road from Portstewart station to Portstewart Town, and four intermediate halts were provided on the short route. The tramway soon became part of the BNCR and passed to the NCC in 1903. Replaced by bus service, it was closed and dismantled in 192. Portstewart station, renamed Cromore, was closed May 1988, although the branch to Portrush remains.

Above: During the last week of working on the Ballycastle line, in July 1950, 2-4-2T No 41 approaches Ballymoney, where once cross-platform connections could be made with the 'Portrush Flier'. The line closed on 3 July and would be finally abandoned by the UTA in 1953. *Ian Allan Library*

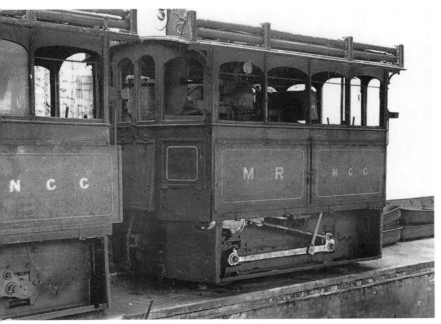

Left: Two Portstewart Tramway engines in store at Belfast York Road shed on 12 June 1937, more than 10 years after closure of the tramway in 1926. It required extensive track renewal and was the first narrow-gauge line in Ireland to be closed by the LMS. No 1, a Kitson 0-4-0T, would subsequently be preserved at Hull, and No 2 at Cultra. *H. C. Casserley*

⑥ Dying days of the Derry Road

What became the 75½-mile Londonderry–Portadown main line of the GNR(I) was constructed in a number of sections. The Londonderry–Strabane section was the first to be opened, in April 1847, by the Londonderry & Enniskillen Railway, and was extended to Omagh and south to Fintona by June 1853. The Portadown, Dungannon & Omagh Railway then completed the route to the towns indicated in its title by 1861, to create the 'Derry Road' from Portadown to Londonderry. The line south to Fintona eventually connected with Enniskillen and Dundalk, providing a service to Dublin and improving the finances of the line. It thus developed as one of the more important routes in Ireland, and the lines all eventually became part of the GNR(I).

A few miles longer than the NCC Belfast–Derry route, the GNR(I) line reached a summit of 561ft in the foothills of the Sperrin Mountains near Pomeroy, while on the picturesque Omagh–Strabane section the River Strule and its tributaries were crossed no fewer than seven times.

The GNR(I) was once a proud, progressive and prosperous company that competed with its coastal rival at its own station at Londonderry Foyle Road. It was also early on the scene with diesel railcars, introducing a number of railcar stops as early as 1936. An extensive timetable of services developed, local services being interspersed with fast trains.

Freight also became important, particularly livestock and other agricultural produce, including milk to the Omagh creamery. Other goods included coal, oil, flax, peat and general merchandise, and such was the growth of traffic that sections of the line were doubled early in the 1900s.

The decline of this main line can be traced back to the partition of Ireland: summertime was not co-ordinated, and Customs checks caused delays, in particular to local Derry–Strabane trains. In 1916 the fastest train took about 2½ hours from Londonderry to Belfast, but by the 1950s 3 hours was a more normal time. From 1935 the railway was also prevented from using its own connecting bus services in Northern Ireland, and this led to buses' being used in direct competition with the railway.

Once the UTA took over it started to run down the line, which was singled throughout. In 1957 the UTA undermined confidence in the route by suggesting that it had no long-term future and simply duplicated the coastal route to Londonderry — despite the fact that it served an entirely different area. The main Portadown–Londonderry line was closed, amidst protest, in February 1965, leaving a gaping hole in the railway map of Ireland. Indeed, almost all the ex-GNR(I) lines west of the Belfast–Dublin main line have been entirely lost.

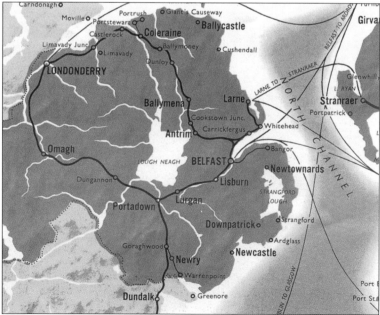

Right: BR map of the 'Derry Road' in 1960. *Author's collection*

Left: The Derry–Enniskillen section of what became known as the 'Derry Road' was planned by Robert Stephenson and eventually became part of the GNR(I). Seen here is Londonderry's Foyle Road terminus (as it was known from 1904), which Italian-styled building, designed by Thomas Turner, would be demolished after closure in 1965. Standing outside the station is a connecting railway bus; at one time there was also a river service linking the station with transatlantic liners calling at Moville. *The Rev J. Parker*

Left: The spacious interior of the GNR(I) Foyle Road station at Derry, looking across the concourse towards the platform barriers; the view is undated, but the time is clearly 11.17am. A single passenger talks to a member of staff while a black dog (in the left-hand corner) looks on. *The Rev J. Parker*

Left: Strabane station on 8 August 1962, with UTA railcar No 101, formerly GNR(I) car A, arriving as the 6.15pm local from Londonderry. The station was still showing signs of damage caused by a hurricane in February 1962. The GNR(I) was very early in the field of diesel railbuses; built as far back as 1932 at Dundalk Works and originally fitted with an AEC diesel engine, this example was later re-engined with a 102hp Gardner diesel. *E. Patterson*

Right: UTA Class U 4-4-0 No 66, formerly GNR(I) No 201 *Meath*, takes water at Strabane while working the 10.15am Londonderry–Belfast Great Victoria Street on 6 August 1964. The locomotive would be scrapped the following year. CDRJC narrow-gauge stock moulders away in the background, the two locomotives visible being 2-6-4Ts No 5 *Drumboe* and No 4 *Meenglas*. N. Machell

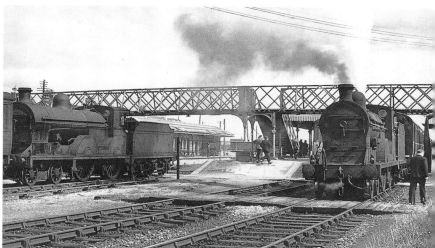

Centre right: Hauled by ex-GNR(I) Class S 4-4-0 No 174, formerly *Carrantuohill*, the 10.15am Londonderry–Belfast train calls at Strabane on 13 July 1964. Shunting wagons on the left is sister No 170, once named *Errigal*. Both locomotives would be scrapped the following year. The trolley crossing was widely used by passengers, and the canopy, damaged by the hurricane, had been repaired. This busy interchange station, once graced by locomotives in beautiful geranium-red CDRJC or sky-blue GNR(I) liveries, would later be demolished. W. Sumner

Below: From 1861 Omagh was the junction for the line to Enniskillen and Clones. Calling on 13 July 1964 is the 10.15am Londonderry–Belfast, hauled by No 174. Note the substantial dumb-bell counterweight on the water crane. The station would be demolished following closure, and the railway alignment is now followed by the appropriately named Great Northern Road. W. Sumner

Table 15   DUBLIN, BELFAST, PORTADOWN, OMAGH and LONDONDERRY—G.N. (Ireland)

Down

Miles		Week Days	Sundays
	Amiens Street ... dep		
	Dublin .... "		
	Belfast B ...... "		
—	Portadown ... dep		
10¼	Trew and Moy ... "		
15	Dungannon .... "		
—	Dungannon ... dep		
23¾	Stewartstown ... "		
29¼	Cookstown ... arr		
24	Pomeroy .... "		
32½	Sixmilecross ..... "		
41¼	Omagh .... arr		
67¾	Enniskillen ... arr		
60½	Strabane .... "		
75¾	Londonderry D "		

Up

	Week Days	Sundays
Foyle Road		
Londonderry . dep		
Strabane .... "		
Enniskillen ..... "		
Omagh .... dep		
Sixmilecross ..... "		
Pomeroy .... "		
Cookstown . dep		
Stewartstown ... "		
Dungannon ... arr		
Dungannon		
Trew and Moy ... "		
Portadown .... arr		
Belfast B .... arr		
Dublin F .... "		

‡ Does not convey passengers for Portadown or Dungannon   § By U.T.A. Omnibus

B Gt. Victoria Street
  Foyle Road
E or $ Except Saturdays
F Amiens Street
Hh Calls on first Wednesday of each month
R Restaurant Car
r Restaurant Car between Portadown & Londonderry
S or $ Saturdays only
Uu Stops when required to take up for stas. beyond Omagh
Vv Calls on Mondays
X or x One class only
Z Calls at certain Public Rd. Level Crossings on request
Zz Calls on Saturdays

Above: Ex-NCC 2-6-0 No 99 *King George VI* takes water at Pomeroy station before commencing the ascent of Carrickmore Bank to the summit of the line with the 11.30am from Belfast on 28 July 1964. The tender held 3,500 gallons of water. Assembled at York Road in 1938 from parts supplied by Derby, the locomotive would be scrapped in 1965. *E. Patterson*

Left: 'Derry Road' timetable, July 1955.

Above: UTA 4-4-0 No 67 *Louth*, formerly GNR(I) No 202, stands at Dungannon with the Saturdays-only 7.25am to Portadown in June 1964. Lack of investment ensured the survival of steam longer on the UTA than in the South. Dungannon had three platforms and was once the junction for the Cookstown branch. The main line would be closed the following year by the UTA, the locomotive being scrapped and the station subsequently demolished. *Y. Strong*

Above right: GNR(I) railcar F, dating from 1938, had four driving wheels coupled hydraulically. It is seen as UTA No 104, waiting at Dungannon after working the 6.35pm Saturdays-only service from Portadown, on 8 August 1964. *N. Machell*

Centre right: Once double-track, the Trew & Moy–Portadown section was singled by the UTA in 1959. This photograph shows single-line staffs being exchanged at Trew & Moy for the 4.40pm Dungannon–Portadown local service on 1 September 1962. UTA Class UG 0-6-0 No 49 was formerly GNR(I) No 149. *J. FitzGerald*

Right: Annaghmore, in the soft boglands south of Lough Neagh, was the first stop after Portadown. Here a UTA railcar set arrives from Portadown in August 1962, but otherwise there is little sign of modernisation. All services on the famous 'Derry Road' would be withdrawn on 15 February 1965. The nearby narrow-gauge Annaghmore turf railway, unique in using electric locomotives, had closed in 1960. *E. Patterson*

7 Donegal dereliction

Weep for the wee Donegal

The County Donegal Railways developed a 125-mile narrow-gauge system, which connected with the Derry Road at Strabane and became the largest narrow-gauge system in the British Isles. The original Strabane–Stranorlar Finn Valley Railway was re-gauged to 3ft by 1894. A narrow-gauge extension to Donegal had opened in 1889, with further branches built with state help to Killybegs in 1893 and to Glenties the following year. The Strabane–Londonderry Victoria Road line opened in 1900, and the branch to Ballyshannon in 1905.

Financial problems led to the formation in 1906 of the County Donegal Railways Joint Committee, which consisted of three members from the Midland Railway's NCC and three from the GNR(I). The GNR(I) refused to subsidise the Strabane–Londonderry section, which competed with its own route, so this section was run by the NCC alone.

The Glenties branch closed in 1947, and the Strabane–Londonderry line was one of the first to be closed by the UTA, in 1955. Although the CDRJC had been progressive under the leadership of Henry Forbes, with its early use of railcars, integrated bus

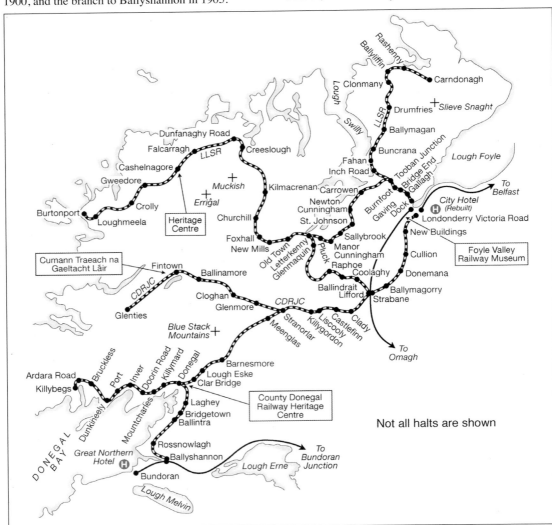

Not all halts are shown

Above: Hauled by CDRJC 2-6-4T *Blanche*, the 12.25pm Letterkenny–Strabane goods calls at Raphoe on 7 August 1959. The lengthy train comprises a mix of freight vehicles, including containers on wagons converted in 1955, which reduced trans-shipment costs and could be Customs-sealed. A single guard's coach can just be seen at the rear. Recorded only a few months from final closure of the railway, the scene reveals a general air of dereliction is beginning to creep in. *K. Pirt*

Right: The closed narrow-gauge side of Strabane station on 12 September 1968, with a CDRJC 2-6-4T dating from 1907 which had been renamed *Drumboe* (ex *Glenties*) in 1937. Although in an ever more derelict state after complete closure of the station, the locomotive was one of four to be saved from being scrapped. Strabane station, after a period of dereliction, was demolished, and today nothing remains. *C. Foss*

services and general improvisation, large-scale track replacement could not be justified, and 1959 proved to be the last full year of operation.

On the last day so many passengers turned up to say farewell that the regular railcar service could not cope, and steam stock was pressed into use. To the sounds of exploding detonators the last passenger train arrived in the drizzle and darkness at Stranorlar, with staff overcome with emotion. With many a tearful eye the CDRJC finally died, although some freight trains ran until February 1960.

After closure the system remained derelict for a while, but demolition began in March 1960. The removal of track left rolling-stock isolated at various locations. *Blanche*, *Phoenix* and railcars Nos 3 and 10 were purchased for preservation by Belfast Museum. Locomotives *Erne*, *Columbkille*, *Meenglas* and *Drumboe* and railcars Nos 12, 16 and 18, together with 10 coaches and 40 wagons and track, were all items intended for preservation in the USA, but high shipping costs precluded trans-shipment, and they remained in an ever-deteriorating condition. In the 1970s the remaining rusting engines and rotting railcars were saved by the preservation movement from further dereliction, but much of the other stock was by then beyond repair.

THE COUNTY DONEGAL RAILWAYS
JOINT COMMITTEE

PUBLIC NOTICE.

On SATURDAY, 26th FEBRUARY, 1921, a number of large boulders were placed on the Railway near Ballinamore Station on the

STRANORLAR & GLENTIES LINE

to obstruct the passage of Trains, and on the same day, and at a point between Fintown and Glenties, a rail was removed, the track was torn up, and so diverted as to result in a Train being thrown off the Line and precipitated down the embankment into the lake alongside. From information received it is clear this was the work of miscreants living in the immediate vicinity.

The action of the cowardly criminals who perpetrated the above might have caused a calamitous accident, and involved the death of the Railwaymen concerned with the working of the Train, as well as the Passengers, and this is to give Notice that if there is any further interference with the Railway the

STRANORLAR AND GLENTIES LINE
WILL BE

CLOSED

For ALL TRAFFIC without further Notice.

Any information that will lead to the identification of the guilty parties will be thankfully received by the undersigned.

HENRY FORBES, Traffic Manager.

STRANORLAR.

Left: Closure notice, a reminder of 'The Troubles'.

Below: Strabane station, once the railway gateway to the CDRJC, on 12 September 1968, after total closure and almost eight years after closure of the CDRJC lines. The Donegal station is on the left, the GNR(I), which closed in 1965, on the right. The locomotive mouldering in the foreground is 2-6-4T *Meenglas*; still rusting at this location in the early 1970s, it would eventually be rescued by preservationists. *C. Foss*

Right: Steam-hauled coaches were retained by the CDRJC for excursion traffic. Two of the 10 coaches purchased by Dr Cox, an American dentist, in 1961 were still to be seen at Strabane in 1965; by this time the track had been removed, and the coaches were not on rails. They had already suffered vandalism, and smashed windows and flaking paintwork hastened the eventual demise of much of this stock. *M. Yardly*

Below right: Stranorlar station bore the coat of arms of Lord Lifford, first Chairman of the Finn Valley Railway; the date 1863, the year of opening, can be seen at the base. Once the hub of the CDRJC, it was photographed in April 1959, the last year of operation. The building would be demolished in 1974, and the ornate crest destroyed. *G. Mahon*

Below: The water tank at Inver, on the Killybegs branch, still holds water in August 2005, some 45 years after closure; the station and goods shed both remain here. Many remnants of the CDRJC lines are to be found: for example, almost all of the Ballyshannon-branch bridges and crossing keepers' houses survive, together with fencing, gates and even the occasional telegraph pole. *Author*

Below right: The only original CDRJC narrow-gauge track remaining is to be found at the old fish pier at Killybegs, seen here in August 2005. Killybegs was an important fishing port, and this line was used to convey fish from the pier. The main station buildings, which were located nearby, have been demolished, the rubble being deposited in the sea to extend the port facilities. *Author*

The Swilly

The Londonderry & Lough Swilly Railway once operated more than 100 miles of line to the remotest and bleakest parts of Donegal. The railway originated in 1863 as a 5ft 3in-gauge line from Londonderry to Farland Point and Buncrana. Opened in 1883, the 3ft-gauge Letterkenny Railway connected with the original line, which was then converted to narrow-gauge. Government-funded extensions opened to Carndonagh in 1901 and to Burtonport in 1903.

The routes were profitable prior to World War 1, and a naval base at Buncrana provided considerable traffic. However, running through such a remote area, they soon began to incur losses. The Buncrana–Carndonagh section closed in October 1935, and the Burtonport extension in June 1940, but a storm of protest over the loss of the route saw all services restored to Gweedore the following year. The Letterkenny–Gweedore section remained open until January 1947, and for specials until June. The Tooban Junction– Letterkenny section continued to be used for freight, and the Londonderry–Buncrana section retained regular passenger trains until September 1948, after which excursions still ran until closure. However, as there were no goods brake vans, freight trains used a passenger brake coach that had a few compartments for passengers wishing to travel over the remaining routes.

Although the LLSR pursued a different path from the CDRJC, turning to road transport early on and failing to modernise, parts of the line were kept alive by subsidies until August 1953 — indeed, the company still survives as a bus operator. Again, after closure dereliction set in until assets were sold off, including the locomotives, which, sadly, were scrapped, but some sturdy remains can still be found, including the quay at Burtonport, many station buildings and parts of Owencarrow Viaduct.

Today County Donegal is without any regular passenger railway but has a wealth of derelict remains.

Left: Letterkenny, the largest town in County Donegal, was where the CDRJC and LLSR systems met, but with the exception of the odd excursion there was little through working, and plans to merge the two systems never came to fruition. The closed LLSR passenger station is seen here on 5 September 1957, at which time the goods yard, reached by a spur from the CDRJC system, was still in use. *N. Simmons*

Left: The sparsely populated glens and mountains of County Donegal were almost exclusively narrow-gauge land. This 1931 photograph shows the end of the LLSR line at Burtonport, with track, signals, engine shed and single pitched-roof signal cabin all looking a bit decrepit, some nine years before closure. The station's passenger buildings still survive today, as do the considerable earthworks. *Ian Allan Library*

Right: Ballyliffin, looking towards Carndonagh, after closure. The station was the second-most northerly station in Ireland — after Rashenny, the next station on the line. Located (like several stations on this railway) some distance from the settlement it served, it was nevertheless used by tourists visiting the nearby sands of Pollan Bay, the platform being extended in 1927. The heavy stone construction of the station house has ensured its survival. *D. Lawrence*

Centre right: Located on the eastern shore of Lough Swilly, the station at Buncrana was very busy in the days of herring fishing. This southward-looking view, recorded following removal of the track, shows the attractive square stone and yellow brick dressings used on the station buildings. The two platforms were at one time joined by a footbridge; this and a turntable once located in the right foreground have gone, but the water tower still remains.
D. Lawrence

Below: Newtowncunningham was the most important intermediate station on the Tooban Junction–Letterkenny stretch of line. Known as simply Newtown, it had two platforms, a substantial station house, goods yard, cattle pens, signalbox and water tower, all remaining when this photograph was taken in 1957. The signalbox has since been removed to the Donegal Railway Heritage Centre. *D. Lawrence*

⑧ Excursions for Warrenpoint

In the 19th century the seaside towns of Warrenpoint and Rostrevor, with their sheltered southerly aspects and surrounding mountain scenery, became important tourist destinations. The Newry, Warrenpoint & Rostrevor Railway opened in May 1849, running some 7 miles from its own terminus at Newry Kilmorey Street, as far as Warrenpoint. The line never reached Rostrevor, but a 2ft 10in-gauge roadside horse-worked tramway did provide a 2¾-mile link to this picturesque resort from 1877 until closure in 1915. The railway became part of the GNR(I) in 1886, and in 1891 that company rebuilt the station at Warrenpoint.

Although Newry was an important port on Carlingford Lough it was destined not to be on the main Belfast–Dublin line, being served instead by a 3½-mile branch from Goraghwood opened in March 1854, and from 1861 links from Kilmorey Street Junction to Dublin Bridge and Edward Street completed a through route from Warrenpoint to the main line. The branch also crossed over the main Belfast–Dublin line and headed north to reach Armagh (by 1864), which, situated on the Portadown–Clones route, thus became a junction for Newry and Warrenpoint.

The Goraghwood–Armagh link crossed a hilly area, and construction required two tunnels, one of which, at almost a mile in length, was the longest in Ireland. Nevertheless, the line was heavily graded, the first mile on leaving Armagh involving a climb at 1 in 82, followed by more than 2 miles at 1 in 75. As it turned out this was to result in tragedy.

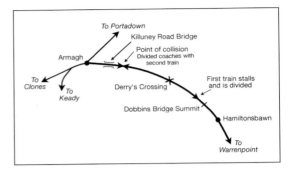

Pleasure trips to the coastal resort of Warrenpoint developed, seasonal day-trippers were welcomed, and excursion trains ran from many inland towns. However, one such excursion was never to reach its destination. On 12 June 1889 the 10am Armagh–Warrenpoint Methodist Sunday School excursion train, heavily loaded with about 1,200 passengers, of whom at least 600 were schoolchildren, stalled on the 1-in-75 gradient south of Armagh, about 200 yards from the summit. It was decided to divide the 15-vehicle train, and stones were put under some wheels of the rear section, it being recognised that,

Below: Armagh station was constructed by the Ulster Railway in 1848 and became part of the GNR(I) in 1876. It is seen here with a GNR(I) train hauled by 4-4-0 No 88, built in 1885. This was the starting-point for the ill-fated excursion to Warrenpoint. *LPC*

apart from the guard's van, the brakes would be inoperative once the vacuum pipe from the locomotive was detached. Unfortunately the stones disintegrated when the engine eased back to allow uncoupling, and the 10-coach detached portion began to run back down the grade. All attempts to re-couple or stop the runaway failed.

The wooden coaches gathered speed and had reached about 40mph by the time they crashed into the engine of the following regular train of three coaches, a horse-box and two vans heading up the grade. The driver of this train saw the runaway and managed to slow to 5mph, and many children were thrown from windows, but in the head-on impact that ensued it is now estimated that 88 eventually died; sadly, more than a quarter were children. Additionally about 400 were injured in a variety of ways. This was the worst accident in Irish railway history and involved the greatest loss of life in any railway accident up to that time. Within days a sad succession of funerals was being held in a stunned Armagh, but the Government was stirred into action to establish binding railway safety regulations.

The Armagh–Goraghwood section continued to be used by passenger trains until 1933, when the Armagh–Markethill section closed completely, the line south to Goraghwood remaining open for goods until 1957. Armagh's last passenger train left in October 1957, and the Goraghwood–Warrenpoint branch closed completely in January 1965, ending rail excursions to Warrenpoint forever.

Several gravestones of those who died in the railway disaster can still be found at Armagh. A commemorative book was published by Armagh Council in 1989 to mark the centenary of the accident.

Above: The worst railway accident in Ireland involved an excursion train bound for Warrenpoint on 12 June 1889. The scene of the disaster, just south of Armagh station, clearly shows the scale of devastation. However, the significance of the accident was such that previously unregulated railway workings ended and compulsory safeguards were soon introduced. *LPC*

Right: Following closure of the Newry–Armagh line to passenger trains in 1933 the principal passenger service to develop was that between Belfast and Warrenpoint. Here the 6.45pm Warrenpoint–Belfast Great Victoria Street train is seen at Newry Dublin Bridge, hauled by ex-GNR(I) Class S 4-4-0 No 60 *Slieve Donard*, on 12 July 1964, during the line's final summer of operation. *W. Sumner*

Above: The 2pm Belfast Great Victoria Street–Warrenpoint train at Newry Dublin Bridge on the same day, behind 'UG' 0-6-0 No 48. One of several level crossings on this section of line at Newry can be seen in the background. Even in the last years trains needed to be strengthened with a considerable number of additional coaches, particularly on Sundays, to cope with the excursion traffic to Warrenpoint. *W. Sumner*

Below: One of the attractive ex-GNR(I) railcars calls at Newry Edward Street station on 6 August 1959. This was the main station in Newry and was located adjacent to the narrow-gauge station of the Bessbrook & Newry Tramway, an electrified 3ft-gauge line that had closed in 1948. *F. Church*

Above right: Still in faded blue livery, UTA Class S 4-4-0 No 60 *Slieve Donard*, formerly GNR(I) No 172, nears Narrow Water Castle with a seven-coach afternoon train on 12 July 1964. The proximity of the line to Carlingford Lough is apparent. *S. Nash*

Right: UTA No 45, an ex-GNR(I) Class UG 0-6-0, passes Narrow Water Castle on a Sundays-only Portadown–Warrenpoint train on 8 July 1962. Narrow Water was the only halt on the line and had been closed in 1958. Much of the railway alignment here has been incorporated into a road. *J. FitzGerald*

Left: An ex-GNR(I) three-car diesel unit, UTA No 114, waits at Warrenpoint on 6 August 1959. Railcars could handle most regular traffic, which included schoolchildren, outside the excursion peaks. The classic William Mills GNR(I)-designed yellow-brick station, with ornate bargeboards and traditional trainshed, is seen here to good effect. *F. Church*

Below left: A busy scene at Warrenpoint station on 12 July 1964: ex-GNR(I) locomotives visible are Class S 4-4-0 *Slieve Donard* (UTA No 60) on the left, a Class UG 0-6-0 (UTA No 48) taking water in the centre and, on the right, Class S 4-4-0 No 171 *Slieve Gullion*, acquired via CIE; the last would subsequently be preserved. This day was a particularly important one in the history of Ulster's transport, and many took the opportunity of an excursion to the coast. *W. Sumner*

Above right: Part of the large and distinctive goods shed at Armagh remained in March 2005. The passenger station, although more ornate, was of a similar style and was located adjacent to this building. *S. Winson*

Right: The imposing iron gates and elegant stone columns of Armagh station are all that remain of the passenger facilities. Built in 1848 by the Ulster Railway and containing four waiting rooms, the station was demolished after closure to passengers in September 1957. Part of the site is now used as a bus depot, as seen here in March 2005. *S. Winson*

⑨ A ghost at Greenore

The LNWR owned the Dundalk, Newry & Greenore Railway, enabling it to extend its operations in Ireland. The English company provided Crewe-built locomotives, and the railway therefore developed very much an LNWR character.

The 12-mile Greenore–Dundalk line was the first to open, in May 1873; passenger ferry services were also provided to Holyhead at the same time. Newry had also been keen to gain access to Greenore, and the 14-mile Greenore–Newry link opened in August 1876. The railway originally had its own station at Newry Bridge Street, but subsequent connecting lines enabled the GNR(I) to run through boat-train services from Belfast. At Dundalk a level crossing of the Dublin–Belfast main line enabled freight to travel westward from Greenore.

Passengers at Greenore were sheltered by a trainshed, and the adjoining hotel, opened in 1873, provided refreshment rooms for the station. A golf course was also made available, in an attempt to promote Greenore itself as a holiday resort, and holiday bungalows were built by the railway company in 1903.

With other ferry routes cutting into its revenue the railway never realised its expectations, but cattle traffic was important. World War 1 interrupted services, and passenger ferries did not resume until 1920. The LMS took over the line in 1923 and ended the operation of passenger ferries after the Britain's 1926 General Strike. The partition of Ireland also affected the line, Customs points being required at Omeath and Greenore. The GNR(I) took over working in 1933, including the hotel, but in 1949 the operation became the responsibility of the UTA, which decided to close the line after 1951. Consequently, on 31 December 1951 thousands turned out along the line on a bleak winter's night to bid farewell to the railway. Bonfires were lit, detonators were exploded, and bands from Newry and Dundalk played 'Auld Lang Syne'.

The hotel also closed its doors on 31 December 1951, since when the building has fallen into gradual dereliction and disrepair. It is said that one visitor looking over the closed building sensed that he was not alone. The reader is left to draw his/her own conclusions about this, but apparently some sort of banshee appeared from nowhere and led the visitor through dusty corridors and crumbling stairs to the top of the building and to a door on to the roof ...

Greenore remained largely unchanged in 2003, when your author visited. There was still a gatehouse to the station yard, and the water tower and the derelict hotel survived, more than 50 years after closure.

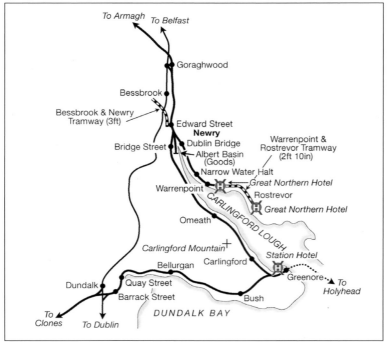

"Could I look round the hotel? I'm writing a book."

"I'll ring up and see, I will at that," came the response from the man at the gatehouse.

He handed over the 'phone, at the other end of which a soft voice replied: "Well, I'd rather you didn't look round — there is not much to see now, and the floors are a wee bit unsafe. I can see you, so I can. I wish you well."

A glance toward the hotel revealed no one. Perhaps it was the ghost of Greenore.

Above: The LNWR was an English company operating in Ireland, and the crest of the LNWR-owned Dundalk, Newry & Greenore Railway incorporated Britannia's hand stretched out across the Irish Sea. The crests and distinctive 'plum and spilt milk' livery of the stock survived until closure of the line, as this view, taken in November 1951, shows. *BR*

Above: The signalbox at Greenore, of broadly LNWR design, stands derelict following closure at the end of 1951. All equipment and track has been removed, but the Greenore Station nameplate is still *in situ*. Much of the original signalling equipment in Ireland was provided by English firms. *D. Lawrence*

Left: Dundalk Greenore boundary marker. *Author*

Right: Ex-Dundalk, Newry & Greenore Railway six-wheeled coaches at Greenore station in August 1951. The coaches were built at Wolverton in 1906 and always ran in LNWR livery. Eight months after closure they remained in the trainshed at Greenore. Legal complications meant that the railway was not finally wound up until 1957. A coach from the railway has been preserved at Cultra. *P. Whitehouse*

Above left: Greenore's empty trainshed, the track having been removed following closure. The refreshment rooms were on the left, while a door to the right led into the Station Hotel and, at one time, to the First-class refreshment room, where a splendid silver restaurant service awaited passengers. *D. Lawrence*

Above: Seen shortly after closure in 1952, Greenore's Station Hotel had survived two world wars and the ending of passenger ferries in 1926. The golf course stayed open after closure of the line, and the railway-built town of Greenore still remains. *D. Lawrence*

Left: The hotel structure survives, albeit in an ever-deteriorating condition. A huge 'HOTEL' sign once graced the upper floor on the right of this August 2003 view. The continuing use of the port is apparent. *Author*

Left: Advertisement for the LNWR's Greenore Hotel, 1910.

10 The Great Northern in life and death

By the 1950s the GNR(I) was making losses, and in 1953 a cross-border Great Northern Railway Board was established. However, in 1958 the GNRB, along with its rolling-stock, was divided between the UTA and CIE. Thus when the UTA closed its section of a particular line CIE had no option but to do likewise with its remaining section in the Republic, and today only the Dublin–Belfast line and a branch to Howth remain in passenger use. Consequently there are many lost lines, and such was the scale of closure that they still evoke vivid memories.

The 'Bundoran Express', one of the few named trains in Ireland, once travelled over 100 miles of railway between Dundalk and Bundoran, a seaside resort on the Atlantic coast. The 88-mile Dundalk–Omagh route was opened by June 1853, and the 35½-mile Bundoran Junction–Bundoran branch in June 1866. Bundoran was originally envisaged as a stop en route to Sligo, but this final section was never constructed, the link with Sligo being provided by a bus service.

The sidings at Belleek provided coal and pottery traffic, but summer tourists were an important source of revenue. In 1899 the GNR(I) opened the Great Northern Hotel at Bundoran to boost holiday traffic on the branch, and in 1934 a number of railcar stops were

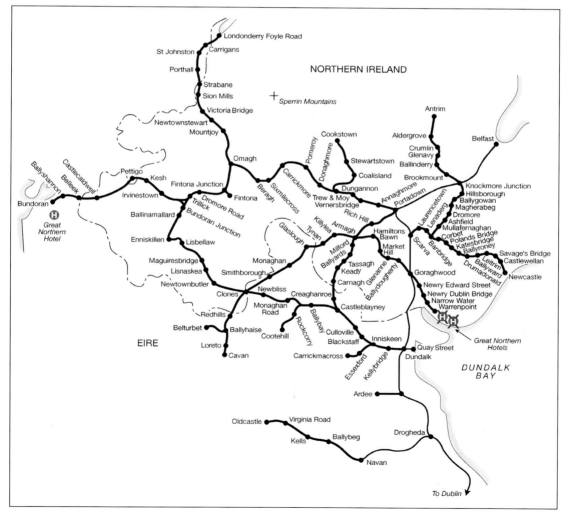

also introduced on the route. Bundoran became a popular seaside resort, and in 1943 the GNR(I) introduced summer expresses from Dublin. The 'Bundoran Express' ran non-stop in Northern Ireland from Clones to Pettigo, thereby avoiding the need for Customs examination at the border stations. Pettigo was a particularly important station for pilgrims to Lough Derg, and connecting buses were provided. However, passenger traffic was light in winter, and the Bundoran line closed in October 1957, together with the links to Clones and Omagh.

There were many junctions on the route of the 'Bundoran Express', but Clones was a major one, at the intersection of two GNR(I) lines — the 121-mile Dundalk– Derry route and the 55-mile Cavan–Portadown line, opened in 1862/3. Clones therefore developed as a railway centre, and in the 1920s the engine shed was rebuilt in concrete as a half roundhouse.

At Cavan the GNR(I) made an end-on connection with the MGWR, which ran south from Cavan some 25 miles to Inny Junction, north of Mullingar. Passenger trains used the MGWR station, which was one of two points of contact between the two railways. In June 1885 a further 4-mile branch from the Clones–Cavan route was opened by the GNR(I) to Belturbet, where it connected with the Cavan & Leitrim Railway.

While the Cavan–Inny Junction section closed to passengers in January 1947, Cavan acted as a bus interchange, and even in 1952 there were four through trains from the county town, via Armagh, to Belfast. Nevertheless the Cavan–Portadown section and link to Belturbet closed to passengers in October 1957; Belturbet closed completely in April 1959. The last lines from Clones, to Dundalk and to Cavan and Monaghan, closed to remaining freight on 1 January 1960.

Left: The 'Bundoran Express' headboard is carried by ex-GNR(I) Class U 4-4-0 No 204 Antrim at Dundalk shed in July 1956. There were few named trains in Ireland, but this was one of the most famous, running from Dublin to Bundoran and including a non-stop section through Northern Ireland to avoid Customs stops. Eight-coach trains were common in the summer. *G. Burton*

Left: At Castleblayney on 31 July 1958 are ex-GNR(I) Class QG 0-6-0 No 154, dating from 1904, and railcar C2, dating from 1935. Three nuns are also to be seen on the platform. This was the junction for the branch line to Armagh via Keady. In terms of passenger service the Keady branch was the shortest-lived on the GNR(I), being used from 1910 to 1923; it had a further claim to fame in that Carnagh was the highest point on the GNR(I). *E. Patterson*

Above: Enniskillen on 5 September 1951, with ex-GNR(I) 'PPs' 4-4-0 No 25 on a Bundoran train. The flat-bottomed rails of the SLNCR track to Sligo diverge to the right, while the corrugated-iron building acted as the SLNCR headquarters office at this station. *E. Patterson*

Left: Another 'PPs'-class 4-4-0, No 50, at the head of a Bundoran–Bundoran Junction train at Ballyshannon in June 1957. There was no physical rail interchange here between the GNR(I) station and the CDRJC narrow-gauge station. Both station buildings still remained in 2005. *L. Nicholson*

Right: A decline in traffic in the 1930s led to the introduction of railcars. Ex-GNR(I) car C1, a Gardiner-Walker articulated vehicle, is seen on 31 May 1957 at Belleek, famous for its pottery; a siding led into the works. Proposals by the UTA to close the Bundoran Junction–Belleek section led inevitably to closure of the entire line. The passenger station at Belleek still survives, and the pottery factory remains open. *M. Jose*

Above: The elegant William Mills design of yellow bricks, decorated with brown and black bricks, was to be found throughout the GNR(I) system, including here at Bundoran *c*1900. An overall trainshed protected the platform behind this modest façade. *courtesy of The Irish Historical Picture Company*

Below: The very last passenger train from Bundoran. The 2.25pm to Enniskillen at the Bundoran platform of the triangular Bundoran Junction station on 30 September 1957. The third side of the junction allowed through Bundoran–Omagh freight and excursion workings. The 'Bundoran Express' did not stop here. *S. Nash*

Above: Clones developed as an important junction on the GNR(I), and there was considerable freight activity, particularly in livestock. Ex-GNR(I) 4-4-0 No 202 *Louth*, UTA No 67, is seen entering Clones station with the 12.10pm train from Dundalk on 11 September 1957. It is clear that electric lights had been introduced to the station's platforms by that time. All remaining services would end in January 1960, the engine shed being used as an industrial site after closure. *N. Shelley*

Below: Cavan North signalbox and the ex-GNR(I) goods yard, seen on 31 July 1958. Cavan passenger station, beyond the goods shed, was divided by a platform-level walkway which marked the boundary between the GNR(I) and the MGWR. Between Clones and Cavan the line crossed the North/South border numerous times, and smuggling was not unknown. *E. Patterson*

Table 14 — DUNDALK, ENNISKILLEN, OMAGH and LONDONDERRY—G.N. (Ireland)

Down	Week Days	Sn	Up	Week Days	Sn
Amiens St.	a.m a.m p.m p.m p.m	p.m a.m	Foyle Road	a.m a.m a.m a.m p.m p.m p.m	p.m
DUBLIN .... dep	8 7 45 9 0 **S** 2 45 4 10	6 25 10 6	Londonderry .... dep	.. .. 6 55 9 35 .. 1 25	**J**
Dundalk .... dep	10 10 10 45 1 30 4 30 6 20	8 10 11 25	Strabane .... "	.. .. 7 36 10 3 .. 2 29	..
Castleblayney ... arr	10 44 11 22 2 10 5 7 6 56	8 48 11 55	Omagh .... "	.. .. 8 25 10 50 .. 4 15	..
Ballybay .... "	10 57 11 40 2 24 5 24 7 19	9 11 12 14	Fintona Junc. .... dep	.. .. 8 20 10 45 .. 4 10	..
Clones .... "	11 22 12 10 .. 5 55 ..	9 40 12 41	Fintona Junc. .... dep	.. .. 8 37 11 3 .. 4 31	..
Monaghan ...... "	.. 1 36 .. 6 48 ..	..	BUNDORAN ...... dep	.. .. .. 7 25 12 25 .. 1 25	..
Armagh .... "	.. 2 29 .. 7 39 ..	..	BALLYSHANNON "	.. .. .. 7 33 12 38 .. 1 41	..
Cavan .... "	.. 1 10 .. 7 5 ..	..	Bundoran Junc. dep	.. .. 9 4 11 28 .. 4 53	..
Maguiresbridge .. "	.. 1 17 .. 6 56 ..	10 23	Enniskillen ..... "	.. 7 20 9 30 12 30 .. 5 14	..
Enniskillen ..... "	.. 1 32 .. 7 11 ..	10 38	Maguiresbridge .. "	.. **a** 9 48 12 42 .. 5 30	..
Bundoran Junc... "	.. 2 28 .. 7 56 ..	..	Cavan .... "	.. 7 35 .. .. 11 20 5 15 ..	..
BALLYSHANNON arr	1 45 3 55 .. 9 22 ..	2 45	Armagh .... "	.. .. 10 5 .. 12 32 5 2 10 56	..
BUNDORAN ..... "	2 0 4 10 .. 9 38 ..	2 58	Monaghan ...... "	.. .. 10 40 .. 1 17 5 42 11 50	..
Fintona Junc.... arr	.. 2 59	..	Clones .... "	.. 8 20 11 5 1 7 3 0 6 25 3 45	..
Fintona .... arr	.. 3 15	..	Ballybay .... "	7 30 8 50 11 38 .. 3 20 6 54 4 15	..
Omagh .... arr	.. 3 11	..	Castleblayney ... "	7 43 9 5 11 57 .. 3 46 7 10 4 29	..
Strabane........ "	.. 4 41	..	Dundalk .... "	8 15 9 40 12 3 .. 4 21 7 40 5 2	..
Londonderry **P**. "	.. 5 5	..	DUBLIN (Amiens St) arr	10 0 11 20 2 45 .. 5 45 9 20 6 32	..

a Calls on request. **J** Not after 14th August. **P** Foyle Road. **R** Restaurant Car.
S or **§** Saturdays only. **X** One class only. **Z** Buffet Car. † Arrival time

Left: Clones/Cavan-area timetable, July 1955.

Left: At Belturbet the GNR(I) met with the narrow-gauge Cavan & Leitrim Railway, and coal from Arigna was transferred laboriously by hand from narrow- to standard-gauge trucks. No 91, the last ex-GNR(I) 2-4-2T in service, is seen in July 1956 by the water tower. Wind-operated pumps provided water to the station from the River Erne until 1925. *G. Burton*

Right: The line to Bundoran crossed the deep gorge of the River Erne at Belleek, by a lattice girder bridge. The girders have been removed, but the stone buttresses on each side remain, as seen here in August 2005. Today the water level under the bridge has been considerably raised by a hydro-electric scheme. *Author's collection*

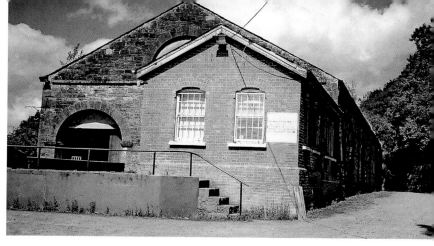

Right: A traditional GNR(I)-style stone goods shed and brick office were built at Cavan, seen here looking north towards Cavan North signalbox. Although closed in 1960, the goods shed was still in occasional use for road freight when this photograph was taken in August 2003. A number of similar buildings remain throughout the ex-GNR(I) network. *Author*

Left: Cavan passenger station has remained largely unchanged since closure. This ticket cabinet at the former station booking office has also survived and was to be seen there in August 2003. The folding sections allowed the wooden cabinet to be closed and locked for security reasons. *Author*

Right: Killylea station, some 15¼ miles from Portadown, was completed in 1859, in an attractive red brick with yellow brick dressings, following the opening of the line by the Ulster Railway. After almost 100 years of use, closure came in 1957, but all the station buildings still survived in 2005, when this photograph was taken. *S. Winson*

Left: At Tynan can be found the remains of the stone-built Ulster Railway station. This section of line was built by William Dargan, but not the stations, leading to a mix of designs. Tynan provided an interchange with the narrow-gauge Clogher Valley Railway, which used this side of the station until closure in 1942; the connecting GNR(I) line was served by two platforms on the other side of the building and finally closed in 1957. The station was in derelict condition when photographed in March 2005.
S. Winson

Left: Tynan signalbox, of classic GNR(I) design, survives in an ever-deteriorating condition, as seen here in March 2005. By 1893 electric block signalling had been introduced on all GNR(I) lines. Tynan was the first station in Northern Ireland for northbound trains from the Irish Republic, and HM Customs checks were once made here. *S. Winson*

Below: The county town of Monaghan boasted impressive station buildings, designed by Sir John MacNeill to replace the original station in 1863. Originally double-track, the line was singled in the 1930s. Eire Customs examinations were once undertaken here also. The passenger buildings survive and are seen here in March 2005 from the road frontage. *S. Winson*

11 Railbus to Sligo

The Sligo, Leitrim & Northern Counties Railway opened the Enniskillen–Carrignagat Junction route, on the main Dublin–Sligo line, in stages from Enniskillen between 1879 and 1882. The line was 42¾ miles long, and running powers into Sligo provided a useful link, particularly for freight, between the MGWR and the GNR(I). The SLNCR was one of Ireland's most distinctive railways and remained independent throughout its lifetime.

Ireland had very limited coal resources, and imported coal was expensive, so experiments with railbuses using other fuels were undertaken much earlier in Ireland than elsewhere. Consequently a number of petrol- and diesel-railbus services were introduced on the line very early on. In 1932 the SLNCR held trials with a railbus to see if economies could be made. It was found that running costs were reduced by 75%, and this led the company to purchase its first petrol railbus in 1934. At that time railbuses were just that — buses fitted with railway wheels — and the first on the SLNCR was an ex-GNR(I) bus converted at Dundalk Works. After a time it was altered to run with a diesel engine, and such was its success that a further similar vehicle was obtained in 1938.

Being normal buses with driving cabs at one end only, the railbuses had to use turntables at each end of the line. Entrance modifications were also required to allow access to platforms on both sides and at track level. Highly distinctive, to today's eye the railbuses can look rather quaint, and they were avoided by many railway enthusiasts, who preferred the steam trains. However, they were popular locally, being seen at the time as a bit of modern and innovative luxury. Although they could lack adhesion on damp, icy or steeply graded rails, a trailer wagon for luggage and parcels was added to most services. A patent was taken out that resulted in the railbuses' running with pneumatic tyres with outer flanged rims of steel for rail use. Furthermore, the railbuses could not be mixed with freight, and improvements to the passenger timetable could be made.

A larger diesel railcar was purchased in 1947 from Walker Bros of Wigan; articulated, this had a separate power unit with driving cab and gave a smoother ride. It also had increased passenger capacity, and cabs at each end gave it a more conventional railcar look. By 1950 most passenger services were operated by railbuses, which were single-class only. However, some steam-hauled stock was retained for mixed trains — notably the 7.20pm from Enniskillen — while other locomotive-hauled stock was kept for excursion trains.

The railbuses had helped the parlous finances of the SLNCR, but closure of the railway was enforced in 1957, as a result of the UTA's stance on adjoining ex-GNR(I) lines. Pleas for a reprieve were ignored, and the line closed with very little notice in October 1957. After closure the larger railcar was sold to CIE and survived in use until 1972; it was subsequently saved from scrap and survives today at the Downpatrick Railway Museum.

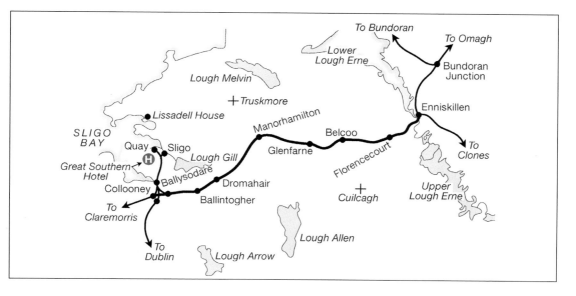

Left: The original railbus, A, was a GNR(I) ADC motor bus converted at Dundalk Works and introduced in 1935. A Gardner diesel engine replaced the AEC petrol original in 1938, but the vehicle's body would be damaged beyond repair in an accident with a steam train the following year. The first railbuses were rather noisy, suffering considerable vibration compared with modern vehicles, but were ideal for reducing costs where there were relatively few passengers using a route. *LPC*

Below left: The replacement railbus A stands at Manorhamilton on 15 September 1948. A 29-seat motor bus converted to run on rails, it used the Gardner diesel engine from the original A. It was fitted with Howden-Meredith patent wheels, consisting of pneumatic rubber tyres encircled with steel rail flanges. *O. Prosser*

Below: The second railbus A, as rebodied *c*1950, operating an Enniskillen–Sligo service at Manorhamilton on 31 May 1954. By this time most passenger services were operated by railbuses, which were painted in an attractive livery of green and cream. Being single-cab vehicles, they had to use turntables at each end of the line. The SLNCR also ran motor-bus services from this station. Note the slotted Saxby & Farmer signal post. *N. Spinks*

Right: Converted from an ex-GNR(I) Leyland motor bus, railbus No 2A was delivered in 1938 and is seen at Dromahair in August 1950. Note the interesting collection of platform facilities. Railbuses stopped at a number of halts not served by steam trains, steps to track level being provided for passengers. No 2A would survive until the line's closure in 1957. *S. Keys*

Right: The Sligo slow coach. Railbus No 2A climbs Glenfarne Bank to Kilmakerrill Summit on 22 June 1955. Due to its wheels' slipping on the wet rails the railbus is making such slow progress that the photographer, a passenger on the train, has been able to get out, run forward and record this view before returning to the vehicle. *P. Gray*

Below: Railcar B forms the 4pm Sligo–Enniskillen service approaching Enniskillen on 2 June 1954. Built in England by Walker Bros of Wigan and placed in service on the SLNCR in the summer of 1947, it had 59 seats, cooling apparatus on the roof and driving cabs at both ends. Note the GNR(I) signal on the left. *N. Spinks*

An article by N. W. Newcombe from *Railway World* in 1960 aptly describes both the romance and the run-down nature of the SLNCR during its last years of operation.

'For me the 7.20pm Enniskillen–Sligo mixed train on the Sligo, Leitrim & Northern Counties will always be the most wonderful train I have ever travelled in. As it stood in the bay platform on 13 April 1957 at Enniskillen, a dull-black but very clean 0-6-4 tank and one elderly reddish-brown composite coach, I sensed that this would be a trip to remember. Inside the coach, apart from leathery seats becoming unstuffed in places, all was bare barren board; but the front compartment was a coupé, with seats on one side only, facing two big windows through which I could see the line ahead, or as much of it as was not obscured by the bunker and cab of *Enniskillen*.

'We pulled out dead on time, and at once reversed to pick up the goods part of our train. I could not tell how many tin cans were attached to the dog's tail, but *Enniskillen* clearly felt her age somewhat when she moved off again; through the windows I saw her pitching, rolling and bouncing like a small ship in a high sea, and guessed that her crew were having a pretty rough passage. The lighting in the coach was somewhat intermittent, and at times it almost went out, but my attention was too concentrated on the way ahead for me to worry about that.

'At Belcoo there were some delighted small boys on the platform to welcome us, and as we stood there in the silence of an Irish evening their bantering to the driver was clearly audible — he seemed to take it in good part. One heard momentarily too the evening songbirds; then the Customs Officer came along, in plain clothes, doing his solemn round. To me he merrily said, "Ah, I've seen you before!" Then off to Glenfarne, where Eire Customs took over, in full uniform this time, but equally cheery and apparently careless about what my haversack may contain.

'On the restart from here *Enniskillen* laboured terribly; she was endearingly like that traction engine in the song that thought she could — and she did. Soon we were belting along in the dusk, a fine moon coming up behind us; it felt like 50-60-70mph, though the sober evidence of my watch said we took 17min 35sec to do the 4¾ miles to Kilmarkerrill, and in cold blood that works out at just over 16mph. I suppose that must be right, but *Enniskillen* was pounding along, wagging her shoulder so furiously that I had doubts whether we should arrive intact at Manorhamilton.

'Our approach to Manorhamilton was very cautious. Not knowing whether the 8.30 in the timetable was meant as an arrival or departure time, I cannot say whether we were 19½ or 26½ minutes late; the 7-minute halt was mainly spent in taking water, but it

Left: SLNCR Notice of Closure, September 1957.

Below: SLNCR timetable, July 1955.

Table 24	ENNISKILLEN and SLIGO—Sligo, Leitrim and Northern Counties										
Miles	**Down**					**Up**					
		Week Days					**Week Days**				
		a m	non	p m	p m		a m	a.m	p m		
		m	m	m	m		m	m	m		
	Enniskillen........dep	6 20	12 0	1 45	7 20	Sligo...........dep	6 20	9 30	4 0		
6½	Florencecourt	6 33	1213	1 58	7 33	Ballysodare........	6 31	9 40	4 13		
12½	Belcoo	6 50	1235	2 18	7 53	Collooney	6 38	9 50	4 20		
17½	Glenfarne........	7 5	1255	2 35	8 10	Dromahair	7 0	1010	4 40	**m** Rail Car, one class only	
24½	Manorhamilton........	7 26	1 15	2 57	8 30	Manorhamilton........	7 25	1030	5 0		
33½	Dromahair........	7 50	1 35	3 17	8 50	Glenfarne........	7 45	1050	5 20		
41	Collooney........	8 15	1 55	3 37	9 15	Belcoo	8 5	1110	5 45		
43½	Ballysodare........	8 25	2 5	3 45	9 25	Florencecourt	8 20	1125	6 0		
48½	Sligo........arr	8 35	2 15	3 55	9 35	Enniskillen ....arr	8 35	1140	6 15		

was prolonged while officials chatted easily. Water dripped mournfully and rhythmically from a sagging hose. In a siding near the station *Lissadell*, a simply Palæolithic 0-6-4 tank, withdrawn two years previously and sold to scrap-merchants who apparently hadn't bothered to come and collect her, stood cold and silent, brooding over the wrongs of aged engines.

'At Dromahair we had a glimpse of the interior of a cottage-shop where the owner seemed to be stocktaking; on the uphill stretches from here into the mountains great travail took place inside *Enniskillen*,

and we enjoyed superb firework displays, with red smoke rolling out of the cab door.

'But before we reached Ballysodare, running now on CIE metals and on the wrong line, as was the custom after the removal of the junction at Carrignagat, we were stopped by signals. I remembered that there was a Dublin–Sligo diesel train due at 9.54. It was only 9.50, but clearly the diesel was to be given the road ahead of our belated caravan. We finally plodded into Sligo station at — let us now be precise, if ever! — 10.27 and 25 seconds. We were roughly 52½ minutes late … but I'd loved it.'

Right: The last two locomotives delivered to the SLNCR were a pair of Beyer Peacock 0-6-4 tank engines which arrived in 1951. The railway's precarious financial position meant that payment was delayed, and eventually it was agreed that the two locomotives could be retained on loan from the manufacturer. Almost new, a gleaming *Lough Erne* is seen in black livery at Enniskillen on 6 September 1951. None of the engines on the line sported numbers — they all had names. *E. Patterson*

Below: The 7.20pm Enniskillen–Sligo mixed train leaves Enniskillen on 1 June 1954 behind 0-6-4T *Lough Melvin*, the other of the final pair of locomotives delivered for use on the line. By the mid-1950s this was the only regular steam-operated passenger service over the route. *N. Spinks*

Above: Belcoo & Blacklion station was the HM Customs point on the line (Irish Customs being located at Glenfarne). *Lough Erne* is seen on 7 September 1957 shunting stock for the 2pm goods for Enniskillen. After closure of the SLNCR the locomotive was sold to the UTA by Beyer Peacock, which until then had remained its owner, and eventually it was preserved. *J. Halliday*

Centre left: The mid-way point on the SLNCR line, Manorhamilton was also the most important intermediate station and the location of the main engineering workshops. Seen on 7 September 1957, just before closure of the line, is composite clerestory bogie brake No 9; 44ft 6in long, it dated from 1924 and was one of three new coaches built to replace eight six-wheelers that had been destroyed in 'The Troubles'. Its maroon livery is fading, and one bogie has been removed for attention. *J. Halliday*

Left: Lissadell, a Beyer Peacock 0-6-4T named after W. B. Yeats's nearby home, was one of five 'Small Tanks' built for the railway between 1882 and 1899.
It was sold to a scrap merchant in 1954, but was still to be seen at Manorhamilton sidings, in a derelict condition, in December 1955. It was to linger until after the line's closure, but none of this type would ultimately survive. *E. Patterson*

13 Dublin broad and narrow

Terminal tales

The main-line railways eventually linked the commercial and cultural centre of Dublin with the rest of Ireland. All had their distinctive termini in the capital. Today a number are closed, though the buildings remain.

Broadstone station was built by the MGWR to an attractive Egyptian style and opened in June 1847. It was the scene of an early railway murder, in 1856, when a railway employee was killed for the day's takings. In January 1937 passenger services on the 1½-mile spur from Liffey Junction to the station were diverted by the GSR into the more centrally located Amiens Street (now Connolly) station. The goods station closed in July 1944, but the line to the engine shed remained in use until 1961, while track on the spur was not removed until 1977.

Harcourt Street station was opened by the Dublin & South Eastern Railway in July 1854 as the terminus of its line to/from Bray, on the coast. The station was situated at the foot of a gradient, and part of it was surrounded by a high stone wall; a spectacular incident occurred in 1900 when the locomotive of a runaway cattle train smashed through this wall and into the adjoining street below, causing considerable damage. The line closed to all traffic in January 1959, but an alternative route to Bray (via the coast) remains, and Dublin's trams use part of the old route.

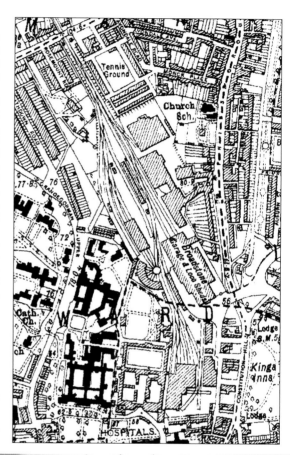

Right: Map of Broadstone station in 1936. *based on Ordnance Survey Ireland Permit No 8018,* © *Ordnance Survey Ireland and Government of Ireland*

Right: Dublin's disused stations have survived remarkably well, enduring 'The Troubles' and 'The Emergency', while the weak state of the economy in the 1960s helped to save them from redevelopment. The magnificent Broadstone station, an Egyptian-styled stone building, designed by John Skipton Mulvany and completed in 1850, was once the hub of the MGWR. However, it was not well located for the city centre, and in 1937 trains were transferred to Amiens Street (now Connolly) station. This photograph was taken in August 2005. *Author*

Left: Ex-GSWR Class J4 0-6-0 No 258 stands beside the turntable in front of the administrative offices at Broadstone on 23 March 1960. At one time new locomotives were built at Broadstone, which was the headquarters of the MGWR. *J. FitzGerald*

Left: On the last day of services from the ex-Dublin & South Eastern Railway Harcourt Street station — 31 December 1958 — the signals are set for the final train, which left at 4.25pm. Large crowds turned out to watch it fade into a foggy afternoon. *Ian Allan Library*

Below left: Map of Harcourt Street station in 1936. *based on Ordnance Survey Ireland Permit No 8018, © Ordnance Survey Ireland and Government of Ireland*

Below: The frontage of the elegant and relatively small terminus at Harcourt Street remains and is seen here in August 2005, complete with the return of the tramlines, in this case using part of the old railway route from Harcourt Street to Stillorgan. *Author*

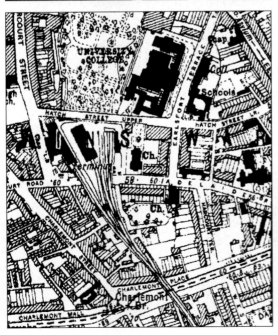

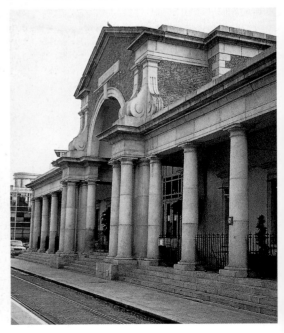

Above: Ex-GSWR 'J4' 0-6-0 No 258 heads a mixed train from North Wall to Kingsbridge (now Heuston) on 27 April 1957. North Wall was also once a key railhead for the export of live cattle to English livestock markets. *H. Davis*

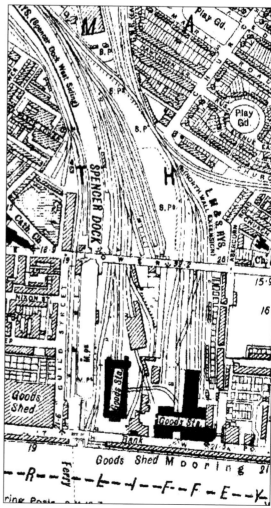

Right: Map of North Wall station in 1936. The closed ex-MGWR goods station at Spencer Dock is on the left, the closed LNWR station on the right. A new Docklands station will soon occupy a small part of this area. *based on Ordnance Survey Ireland Permit No 8018, © Ordnance Survey Ireland and Government of Ireland*

North Wall

The importance of Dublin North Wall, at the mouth of the River Liffey, as a port facility was recognised by the railways. The LNWR had facilities at Dublin to support its shipping services, including a passenger station opened at North Wall in 1877. The Holyhead–Dublin link developed as the most important Anglo-Irish route, and the LNWR promoted its station, although passenger trains were provided by other railway companies. The LNWR also provided an adjacent hotel, opened in 1885. The area around Dublin was most important for beef cattle, and vast quantities of livestock were exported from the docks. Livery stables and even a garage were also once provided by the LNWR.

The 1919-21 war between Ireland and Britain did nothing for an English-owned railway in Dublin; passenger services had ceased by the end of 1922, and the hotel closed the following year. Part of the LNWR passenger station still survives, as does the hotel, now used as offices.

Left: The LNWR's North Wall station opened in 1877, and regular passenger services ran until 1922. The station building continued in use for freight services on the North Wall, and a container depot that used part of the ex-LNWR yard closed in May 2001. Shorn of its exterior canopy, much of the station was still in existence when this view was recorded in August 2005. *Author*

Below left: The North Western Hotel was opened by the LNWR in 1885 and boasted a tranquil garden in the dock area. During 'The Troubles' it housed a battalion of the 'Black & Tans', who remained until the truce of 1921. Trade never recovered, and it was closed by the LMS in 1923. The attractive building is seen here in use as railway offices in August 2005. *Author*

Below: Although standard-gauge shunters, including Guinness-owned locomotives, were used in the Guinness Kingsbridge exchange sidings, this view shows shunting operations being undertaken by a Guinness narrow-gauge engine mounted on a standard-gauge haulage wagon. This slow but powerful contraption enabled the 1ft 10in-gauge engines to work on 5ft 3in-gauge lines. Opened in 1875, the exchange sidings were to close in May 1965. *Ian Allan Library*

Right: The scene at Victoria Quay, on the River Liffey, as barrels of Guinness are transferred to barges for export. Two lines once linked the brewery to the quay area, but the quay and the section of narrow-gauge railway that served it closed in April 1961. Although the famous stout remains, the quay was demolished in 1963. *Guinness Archive, Diageo Ireland*

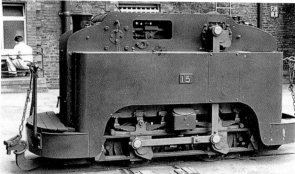

Right: Designed by Samuel Geoghegan and built in Dublin by William Spence in 1895, 1ft 10in-gauge 0-4-0T No 15 is seen at the St James's Gate brewery of Arthur Guinness & Sons on 10 May 1962. The design of the locomotives working the brewery lines was unique: restricted to the size of the horses that had originally worked the line, they had their cylinders above the boiler, with vertical connecting rods leading from the upper crankshaft to the wheels. Withdrawn in 1957, No 15 is one of a number to have been saved from scrap. *Ian Allan Library*

Liffey water

Liffey water is used to make a famous stout, and the Guinness brewery at Dublin once had the largest industrial railway in Ireland. Much of the 1ft 10in-gauge system was constructed between 1873 and 1877, and it eventually comprised an 8-mile network. Some lines were located in public streets, linking the brewery to the main-line exchange sidings and to a quay on the River Liffey. To avoid the need to reverse trains the layout included numerous triangular junctions — a forerunner of the 'merry-go-round' principle. The line also included a spiral tunnel, 865ft long, comprising more than two and a half turns on a 1-in-39 gradient, enabling it to link the two levels of the brewery.

The system was eventually worked by a fleet of Dublin-built narrow-gauge locomotives, unique in that they could be hoisted onto a standard-gauge truck and used to drive it along; this innovative contraption, used on the standard-gauge sidings, was slow but powerful. Diesel traction eventually replaced steam, but steam locomotives remained on standby until 1964. The link from Kingsbridge yard to the brewery's interchange sidings was closed in May 1965, the remaining narrow-gauge brewery lines following in August 1975.

Views of Dublin in James Joyce's day invariably featured the city's extensive tramway system. Today Dublin has brought the trams back. North Wall is still operational in part for freight, while the Guinness brewery remains in operation — *sláinte!*

Above: Sections of the extensive narrow-gauge system at the Guinness brewery remain, as can be seen here in August 2005. The web-and-flange 76lb steel rails were laid in granite to minimise surface disruption to road vehicles. Several items of rolling-stock have also been preserved. *Author*

14 A trio of tramways and tractions

Steam to Blessington

The Dublin & Blessington Steam Tramway was built as a result of the Light Railways Act of 1887 and opened in August 1888. The Terenure terminus, on the outskirts of Dublin, was served by the city's tram system. As with the Dublin & Lucan Tramway, the track followed the road for most of its length. However, the numerous crossings and, in some cases, central-road running led to so many fatal accidents that the line was sometimes known as 'the longest graveyard in Ireland'.

In 1895 an extension to Poulaphouca was opened, resulting in a 20¼-mile standard-gauge route from Dublin. The tramway was well used prior to World War 1, and an army camp provided considerable revenue, troops being marched the 5 miles from Brittas station to the camp. Mail was also conveyed on the line, together with agricultural produce. The route was also promoted as the cheapest and most picturesque line to the Punchestown horse trials.

A letter to the *Dublin Evening Telegraph* in 1911 called the tramway the 'Scrap Iron Express'; when the

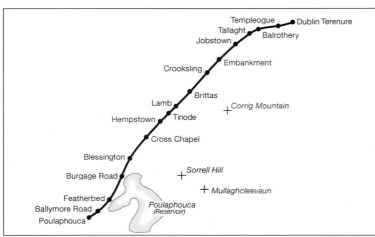

Above: Dublin & Blessington Steam Tramway 0-4-2T No 8, built by Green of Leeds in 1896. The engine had controls at both ends, a high chimney (to reduce smoke emissions for the adjoining coaches) and electric lights for street working. It would be scrapped in 1915. *LPC*

writer had asked what time his train would arrive at Terenure, an official had apparently replied: 'Oh, it would take a smarter fellow than me to tell you that — we might be there at the scheduled time, we might be there in the small hours and we might not arrive at Terenure at all.' Enquiring why the directors did not do anything about such a state of affairs, the correspondent was informed that they were getting 'their bit' out of the tramway whether it paid or not, as the local council levied a rate to keep the line running.

Decline came after World War 1; the army camp was wound down, and for a time opposing sides in 'The Troubles' blocked the line. Two railcars were purchased but proved unreliable, and most services remained steam-operated to the end. Electrification was considered, but the Blessington–Poulaphouca section closed in September 1927, the remaining section following at the end of December 1932. The two railcars were sold to the CDRJC and were re-gauged in 1934; one survived and is preserved at Cultra.

Above: From 1926 a Drewry railcar was used on the tramway. It had 40 seats and a peculiar wheel arrangement — two large pairs flanked by two smaller pairs. Following closure of the tramway it was eventually sold to the CDRJC in 1934 and in 1942 was rebuilt as a trailer, being seen here as CDRJC car No 3 on 18 September 1947. *S. Keyse*

Right: Poulaphouca station was opened in May 1895 by the nominally independent Blessington & Poulaphouca Tramway, which was worked by the Dublin & Blessington Steam Tramway. The roadside terminus, some 5 miles from the Blessington, was the first section to close, in 1927. The former station was being used as a private residence when photographed in August 2003. *Author*

Left: Ex-GNR(I) 5ft 3in-gauge Hill of Howth tram No 4 approaches, as the trams prepare to pass on the single-line route. Fine views were available from the upper decks of the open-top electric tramcars as the line climbed to its 407ft summit. The single tram poles and overhead electric wires are apparent in this 1950s photograph. *Ian Allan Library*

Left: Tram No 5 at Hill of Howth station. This was one of an original batch of eight cars supplied by Brush of Loughborough and painted in GNR(I) railcar blue and cream livery. The line, with more than two dozen stops, was to close in May 1959, the last tram system in Ireland, but four of the trams would be saved from scrap. *Ian Allan Library*

Howth electrics

The Hill of Howth attracted Dubliners to the picturesque headland and sea views, and a tramway was opened by the GNR(I), with tourism expected to be the principal source of traffic. The Sutton–Hill of Howth section opened in June 1901, and the Hill of Howth–Howth link in August that year, providing a 5¼-mile horseshoe route. At both Sutton and Howth the tramway connected with trains on the GNR(I) Howth branch.

The 5ft 3in-gauge line climbed at gradients as steep as 1 in 16½ from Sutton to the Hill of Howth, where fine views across Dublin Bay were to be enjoyed from the open-top double-deck trams. After reaching the summit the line curved north and again provided excellent views over Howth harbour and its fishing fleet. The line was electrified at 550V DC, with double-deck open-top trams working all services. The tram service was withdrawn with just two weeks' notice in June 1959, although the ex-GNR(I) branch to Howth remains open.

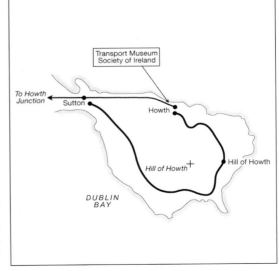

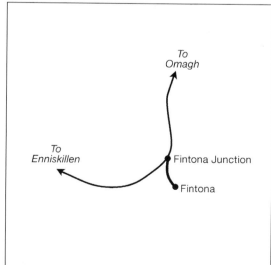

To Omagh

To Enniskillen

Fintona Junction

Fintona

Horse to Fintona

Opened in 1853, the three-quarter-mile 5ft 3in-gauge line ran from Fintona Junction, on the Omagh–Enniskillen line, to Fintona itself. It was a short but famous line, which for many years typified the variety of Irish rail travel. For its entire existence the passenger service was horse-drawn, but freight was steam-hauled. The double-deck horse-drawn tram made connections with GNR(I) trains at Fintona Junction.

Although the service was an anachronism long before closure, the unique tram was the pride of the GNR(I), and certainly this hay-powered line never had problems during any fuel crisis.

The gradient was uphill from Fintona to Fintona Junction, and progress in this direction was slower than on the descent to the town. Average speed was generally around 6mph; indeed, it was said that a brisk walk could beat the tram to the station. This last horse tramway in the British Isles closed on 1 October 1957; the horse, Dick, was put out to grass, while the tramcar is preserved at Cultra.

Achill

The 27-mile westerly extension of the MGWR, from Westport to the Atlantic coast at Achill, did not cross Achill Sound to the island itself. It was opened throughout in May 1895 by the Board of Works, which subsidised construction costs, and was routed through a rugged area; although it had significant gradients, it was substantially built.

Three trains each way served this isolated area, one providing a through coach to/from Dublin — a journey of some 187 miles — which ran until the line closed. The scenery was spectacular and a MGWR hotel was built at Mallaranny in 1897. There was agricultural freight, some fish traffic and mail, but such a remote area, economically depressed and sparsely populated, generated little revenue.

The line enjoyed some seasonal tourist traffic, and a petrol railcar was tried out, but this could not prevent closure by the GSR in 1935. The resultant uproar led to its reopening the following year while road improvements were made, final closure being

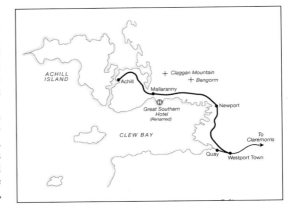

implemented in October 1937. The hotel at Mallaranny (also spelt Mulranny) is still in use, and several remains of the railway, including viaducts and tunnels, are also to be found, more than 60 years after closure.

Left: Achill station, terminus of the line from Westport, *c*1900. The opening had been spurred on by a disaster in 1894, when a boat providing the Achill link sank, drowning all on board. The line's closure would be even more heartbreaking, the last passenger train from Westport bringing home the coffins of 10 Achill children killed in a barn fire while harvesting potatoes in Scotland. The Achill station nameplates are preserved at Hell's Kitchen Railway Bar and Museum in Castlerea. *courtesy of The Irish Historical Picture Company*

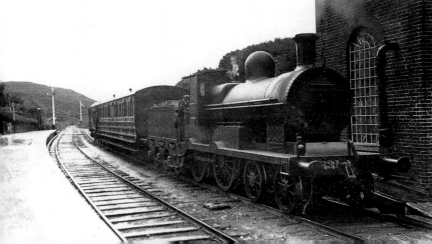

Left: Ex-MGWR rebuilt 4-4-0 *Cyclops*, renumbered 531 by the GSR, calls at Mallaranny station on a 'soft' day in the 1930s. The omens are not good: beautiful scenery, but no passengers. The MGWR hotel built here boosted tourism on the line and survives long after the railway, John Lennon having been one of its more famous guests. *LPC*

Right: The southern end of the damp 133yd Newport Tunnel, on the Westport–Achill branch. The MGWR line opened as far as Mallaranny in 1894, with the help of public funds supplied by the Baronies, later known as councils. Such publicly funded routes were sometimes known as Baronial lines. *L. Goulder*

Ballaghaderreen

The town of Ballaghaderreen was the terminus of the 9-mile branch line from Kilfree Junction, on the Dublin–Sligo line. The branch was opened in November 1874 by the nominally independent Sligo & Ballaghaderreen Junction Railway but was worked from the start by the MGWR. It closed in January 1947 due to the fuel shortage, but services resumed in May of that year.

An intermediate station was provided at Edmondstown, a second being added in 1909 at Island Road. Ballaghaderreen itself was a market town, and livestock was an important source of freight on the branch. For most of its life the line used a mixture of old and very old stock, and it became one of the last

CIE lines to be regularly operated by steam. Timings were slow, but the coaches were clean and the staff friendly. The branch and Kilfree Junction closed to all traffic in February 1963.

Right: An ex-MGWR 2-4-0 (CIE No 655) in a poor state of repair at Ballaghaderreen with the three-coach branch passenger train in September 1960. The view gives an indication of the lack of railway investment at that time. *L. Nicolson*

Below: Ballaghaderreen–Kilfree Junction timetable, April 1910.

	KILFREE JUNCTION and BALLAGHADERREEN.—Midland Great Western.												
Miles	**Down.**		**Week Days.**				**Miles**	**Up.**		**Week Days.**			
		mrn	aft	aft	aft				mrn	aft	aft	aft	
	Kilfree Junction ....dep.	1030	1 22	4 50	8 45	....		Ballaghaderreen . dep.	9 30	1235	3 30	7 45	....
7	Edmondstown	1050	1 38	5 6	9 1	....	2	Edmondstown	9 38	1243	3 38	7 55	....
9	Ballaghaderreen....arr.	1059	1 45	5 13	9 8	....	9	Kilfree Junc. 912 arr.	9 53	1259	3 53	8 14	....

Left: The 11.50am Ballaghaderreen–Kilfree Junction mixed train, hauled by an ex-MGWR 0-6-0, CIE No 574, on 31 July 1962. Plans for Ballaghaderreen to be on a through route never came to fruition. Most journeys involved changing trains at Kilfree Junction, although some excursions ran direct to Sligo. *E. Patterson*

Right: Operating the Ballaghaderreen branch on 12 September 1962, CIE No 654 was one of a batch of 2-4-0 locomotives introduced on the MGWR by M. Atock between 1893 and 1898 and later known as the 'G2' class. This was one of the last steam-worked branches in Ireland, while the locomotives were among the last 2-4-0s working in the British Isles. *M. Esau*

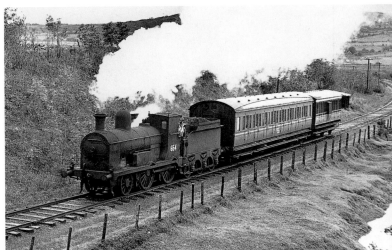

Left: Hauled by ex-MGWR 0-6-0 No 610, the afternoon mixed train from Attymon Junction arrives at Loughrea on 26 July 1960. The branch was another of Ireland's Baronial lines, built with public money. The stone station buildings still remain. *E. Patterson*

Loughrea

The small town of Loughrea was served by a 9-mile branch line from Attymon Junction, on the Galway–Dublin main line. The branch opened in December 1890 as a standard-gauge line, built as a light railway under the terms of the 1883 Act.

Passenger services were suspended in February 1947 due to the fuel shortages, and goods services were also suspended the following month. Freight resumed in May and passengers the following month, although many trains were mixed, and some remained so until the line's closure.

Having narrowly escaped being axed in 1962, the line closed completely in November 1975. This was the last truly country branch passenger service to close in the British Isles. The rusting track was initially retained pending the line's possible reactivation as a tourist railway but was lifted in 1988.

Your author made a trip over the line in August 1973, as the following diary extract reveals:

'I arrived at Attymon Junction to find the Loughrea branch train waiting, consisting of a single coach hauled by B209. It had been said that the coach was heated by a night-storage heater now that steam was not used, and sure enough it was, but fortunately the heating was not on, it being August, although they said the mornings could still be cool.

'I asked the driver if I could have a ride in the cab. "No problem," he beamed, and we soon set off towards Loughrea. The springing on the engine was very hard, and we bounced about on track that looked astonishingly light. The stop at Dunsandle allowed a single passenger to alight and we were off again to

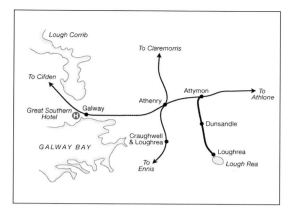

Loughrea.

'On arrival the driver reversed to the front of the train, leaving the engine for the morning. I encouraged the friendly staff to pull the signal "on" and "off" for my cine film. I also noted cattle wagons at the station, although the goods shed was derelict. It was late, but a hotel by the station had a room for the night and I walked to see the sun set over Loughrea, ending a perfect day.'

Below: Loughrea–Attymon Junction timetable, April 1910.

Bottom: Deutz 0-4-0 diesel-hydraulic No G615 at Loughrea with a train for Attymon Junction on 1 April 1963. The 160hp engine was part of a cost-cutting experiment to see if one-man-operated diesel locomotives could be used on the light track of country branches; its success resulted in the reopening to freight of the Castleisland and Newmarket branches, which were to survive for a number of years before final closure.
R. Joanes

ATTYMON JUNCTION and LOUGHREA.—Midland Great Western.

Miles	Down.		Week Days.							Miles	Up.		Week Days.						
		mrn	aft	aft	aft								mrn	aft	aft	aft			
	Attymon Junction..dep.	1030	1 25	158	12	...	...	...	...		Loughrea............dep.	9 25	1220	3 35	7 10	...	...	...	...
4	Dunsandle.............	1049	1 14	5 27	8 24	...	...	...	...	5	Dunsandle.............	9 39	1234	3 49	7 32	...	...	...	...
9	Loughrea........ ..arr.	11 3	1 25	5 38	8 35	...	...	...	...	9	Attymon Junction 911 arr.	9 50	1245	4 0	7 46	...	...	...	...

Mitchelstown

Constructed as Light Railway, the 12-mile Fermoy–Mitchelstown branch was opened in March 1891. Part of the GSWR from 1900, it developed a service of five weekday trains to/from the main line at Fermoy, where connections were once provided with Cork–Rosslare boat trains. Perhaps the 13 non-station crossings on the branch proved unlucky, for passenger services ceased in January 1947. The remaining freight trains, mainly livestock specials, were withdrawn by the end of 1953.

The main-line connection at Fermoy, on the 75-mile Mallow–Waterford line, itself closed in 1967, although a short eastern section has reopened as the narrow-gauge Waterford & Suir Valley Railway.

Above: Metropolitan-Vickers/GM Bo-Bo diesel-electric No 223 arrives at Dunsandle with the 11.40am train to Loughrea. The only intermediate station on the branch, Dunsandle originally had a loop and ballast sidings, but facilities had been reduced to a single siding by the time this photograph was taken on 27 August 1974, during the last summer of operation. *A. Dale*

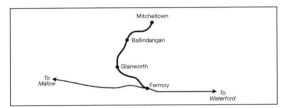

Above: Fermoy station on 28 March 1963, with Metropolitan Vickers Co-Co diesel-electric No A11 at the head of a goods train and General Motors Bo-Bo No B141 on a passenger train for Cork; on the right is preserved ex-GSWR 0-6-0T No 90, dating from 1875. The last, which still survives, was to be found here because the Mitchelstown branch had been worked from this platform by two similar locomotives. *R. Joanes*

Left: Ex-GSWR Class 2 'Kerry Bogie' 4-4-0 No 15 at Mitchelstown in 1931. This class, built between 1877 and 1880, was used for branch and cross-country work. Note the distinctive double-folding smokebox doors. Like many Irish steam locomotives they were long-lived, some surviving until 1957. Mitchelstown station was located above the town, on rising gradients from Fermoy. There are no remains there today other than a gate and a few foundations in a remote field. *Ian Allan Library*

Above: Opened in 1860, the substantial junction station at Fermoy survives, complete with the overall roof behind the station house, as seen here in May 2005. The last train left in 1967, almost 15 years after the closure of the Mitchelstown branch. *Author*

Tramore

From September 1853 the single line of the Waterford & Tramore Railway ran the 7¼ miles from Waterford Manor station to the popular coastal resort of Tramore. There were no intermediate stations, but both termini were substantial and elegant buildings, with overall roofs. The line was economically run and prospered for many years, although plans to link the isolated line with the main network (by means of a tunnel at Waterford) were never fulfilled. Like all the branches described in this chapter the line was taken over by the GSR in 1925. Even as late as 1953 trains ran 17 hours a day in the summertime peak, and every item of rolling stock was pressed into service.

Diesel railcars had replaced steam by 1955, but in spite of this modernisation it soon became clear that CIE intended to substitute buses on the route. The line was closed on 31 December 1960 and lifted the

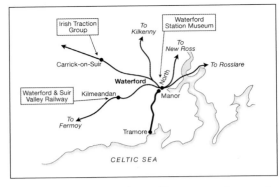

following year. The station at Tramore survives, as do a number of bridges on the line. Little remains at Waterford, although a museum at the IÉ station recalls the route.

Above: For many years the Tramore branch was worked by 2-2-2WTs built by Fairbairn in 1855. They became the last single-wheeler engines to remain in the British Isles, and No 1, seen at Waterford Manor early on in the line's history, would last until 1935, ultimately being scrapped following a derailment. Note the ornate trainshed and the high windows of the coach. The station has been demolished, but Railway Square remains, and new trees have been planted. *Ian Allan Library*

Left: The substantial and distinctive disused station at Tramore. An ornate trainshed used to cover the single platform, while Jacobean architectural influences are to be found in the brick-and-stone building, which was for sale when photographed in August 2005. *Author*

16 Coal on the Cavan & Leitrim

The Cavan, Leitrim & Roscommon Light Railway & Tramway was incorporated under the terms of the 1883 Light Railways Act, assuming the shorter Cavan & Leitrim title in 1895. The 33¼-mile main line opened in October 1887, the 14¾-mile Arigna branch in May of the following year.

This was a rural area: two slaughterhouses were located on the route, and milk was carried to creameries on the line. Parcel traffic and mail were also conveyed. In 1897 connecting steamer services were introduced on the River Shannon from Dromod, but these proved uneconomic and were withdrawn in

1904. Summer excursions provided extra revenue, but this was a remote area with little population or commerce.

Coal became the most important freight on the line. The Arigna area was the location of some of Ireland's few coal mines and already supplied the line's locomotives. World War 1 gave the mines renewed importance, and a logical 4¼-mile extension to the coal pits was at last agreed, the new line using part of the formation of the old Arigna Iron Works Tramway, dating from 1830. Consideration was given to the use of transporter wagons (as on the Leek & Manifold

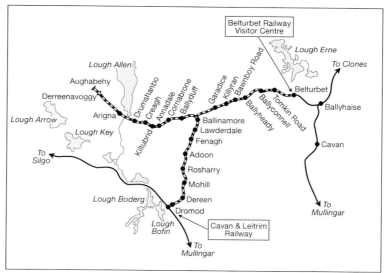

Below: Hunslet-built 2-6-0T No 6T, dating from 1889, heads an empty coal train on the 4½-mile tramway extension between Arigna station and the coal mines on 6 August 1957. The 'T' suffix indicated that it came from the Tralee & Dingle Railway, this being one of the first two ex-TDR locomotives to run on the CLR. It had also been used for a while on the West Clare line, losing its bell and cowcatcher. It would survive until closure of the CLR, being then scrapped. *A. Donaldson*

narrow-gauge railway in England), but insufficient clearance meant that stock borrowed from the NCC lines was used when the extension opened in June 1920.

'The Troubles' resulted in problems for the railways. In 1923 some 900 men of the Northern Command of the Free State Army, intent on invading high ground held by Republican forces, were conveyed by special train to Arigna; here they boarded wagons to travel on to Derreenavoggy — the only passengers ever to use this section of line.

Demand for coal reached its peak in 1926, during Britain's General Strike, when even cattle wagons were pressed into use to convey the low-grade coal. Yet, overall, traffic never matched expectations, and by 1930 the line beyond Derreenavoggy was closed. However, an aerial ropeway connected other mines to Derreenavoggy, and traffic on the remaining extension revived. During World War 2 — known in Eire as 'The Emergency' — the mines once again became vital, and coal traffic continued after the war.

In February 1947 snow disrupted services, but the line nevertheless came to 'The relief of Drumshanbo', which town (incorrectly spelled at the station as 'Drumshambo') had been cut off for a week by the time a double-headed train equipped with a snowplough managed to batter its way through the drifts with much-needed supplies.

In 1956 the railway won a contract to transport 300 tons of coal a day. Overall traffic was high, and locomotives from closed narrow-gauge lines were drafted in to help operate the coal trains. However, early in 1959 a leaflet appeared announcing closure. Locomotives, stock and track were worn out, and the cost of modernisation was considered prohibitive.

Although only one original CLR engine was serviceable, the last two days of the line saw extra trains provided for locals and enthusiasts to say farewell to the railway, which had become a veritable museum of engines and stock transferred from other narrow-gauge lines. It was also the only narrow-gauge railway in Ireland worked throughout its lifetime by steam, and CLR locomotives Nos 2 and 3 survived into preservation.

After the line closed, in March 1959, the track was gradually lifted, and some buildings were allowed to fall into disrepair. In 1994 a preserved section reopened at Dromod, with plans to extend 5½ miles to Mohill, while at Belturbet the former GNR(I) interchange station has also been restored.

Below: 2-6-0T No 4T came to the line in 1941, the first of two ex-TDR locomotives to assist with working the coal specials, which were so important during 'The Emergency'. It is seen in Ballinamore station with a coal train from the Arigna mines on 4 June 1957. Original CLR wagons carried 5 tons of coal, but later wagons could transport 6 tons; 10 wagons was the maximum usually allowed on the tramway. Ballinamore was the main junction on the line and the hub of the system. *L. Nicolson*

Above: 4-4-0T No 2L at Cannaboe level crossing, approaching Ballinamore station on 5 June 1957 with a coal train from Arigna; the 'L' denoted the GSR Cavan & Leitrim section of line. The locomotives all lost their names when the GSR took over in 1925. The line on the left ran to Dromod. Today 'The Arigna Mining Experience' provides a tour of what was Ireland's last working coal mine, which closed in 1990. *L. Nicolson*

Centre left: Locomotives from the Cork, Blackrock & Passage Railway were first sent to the CLR in 1934. Ideal for Cork suburban trains, they were less suitable and rather ungainly on heavy coal trains, particularly on Lawderdale Bank. They were also banned from the tight curves of the tramway extension, but overall they gave good service on the line and were worked to death before closure of the line. 2-4-2T No 10L is seen at Ballyconnell on 6 September 1951. *G. Burton*

Left: 4-4-0T No 2L simmers in the yard at Ballinamore shed on 4 June 1957. The original CLR locomotive was rebuilt in 1940 at Inchicore Works with the cab, tanks and boiler from No 7. Although the system was neglected, loyal staff at Ballinamore used a mixture of skill and improvisation to keep the engines going. *L. Nicolson*

Left: 0-6-0T No 4T outside the wagon shop and store at Ballinamore on 4 June 1957. This ex-TDR locomotive was well employed on the CLR and would be used for lifting the line. The running shed is on the right and the water tank in the background (right). The site is now a school, the former wagon shops being used as classrooms. *L. Nicolson*

Below: Ballinamore station after removal of the track. Trains ran for 10 days after the official closure date in March 1959 to clear all the traffic. The track here was lifted shortly after closure, but the Arigna tramway extension remained *in situ* until 1964. *D. Lawrence*

Left: Mohill station after the removal of the track. The station buildings were similar to those on the down platform at Dromod, but three (rather than two) gables were used for the station house. The buildings and gardens still survive, and plans are in hand to restore the section of line between here and Dromod. *D. Lawrence*

17 **Steam specials**

The excursion train has always been an important feature of Ireland's railways. Steam-hauled excursions enabled railway enthusiasts to make last journeys over lines that were to close, and this chapter records a number of such excursions and the lines over which they once travelled.

Antrim

The 18½-mile Knockmore Junction–Antrim line opened in November 1871 and became a key route of the GNR(I), joining the NCC Belfast–Derry line at Antrim. A siding to Aldergrove Airport was opened in 1916 but closed at the end of World War 2. The main line was busy during the war and in June 1944 was used by some 52 troop and 88 wartime goods trains. The line was closed to passengers by the UTA in September 1960 but was reopened by NIR to local

traffic in January 1974 and to Belfast–Derry trains in January 1978. In June 2001 the Derry services were diverted via the reinstated Bleach Green Junction, on the ex-NCC Antrim line. Consequently this ex-GNR(I) section closed in June 2003 — the first major closure in Northern Ireland since 1965. However, the track has been 'mothballed' pending use as part of a proposed Belfast–Lisburn–Antrim–Belfast circle line.

Below: Ex-GNR(I) 'S'-class 4-4-0 No 171 *Slieve Gullion*, built in 1913 and preserved by the RPSI, approaches Crumlin Viaduct on the old GNR(I) Knockmore Junction–Antrim route with the 'Sorley Boy' railtour of Saturday 31 May 1969. Several lattice girder bridges of this general design are to be found in Ireland. Closed in 2003, the track remains *in situ. A. Stewart*

Left: CIE No 132, an ex-GNR(I) 'Q'-class 4-4-0, at Kingscourt on 3 June 1961 with an Irish Railway Record Society tour of Co Meath lines. Plans by the MGWR to extend the line northward from Kingscourt never proceeded. Passenger trains ceased in 1947, but gypsum traffic would continue until 2001.
J. FitzGerald

Left: Hauled by preserved GSWR No 186, the 'Royal Meath' railtour passes Nobber, on the ex-MGWR Kingscourt branch, on 23 May 1970. The station had closed to passengers in 1947, and the line would succumb in 2001, but the rusting track still remained in 2006.
A. Donaldson

Royal Meath

The 43½-mile MGWR branch line to Kingscourt ran north from Clonsilla, on the Dublin–Sligo line, and was opened throughout by November 1875. Passenger services were never reinstated after the fuel shortages of 1947, and the Clonsilla–Navan section closed to remaining freight in April 1963; thereafter all freight trains to/from Kingscourt travelled via the ex-GNR(I) Drogheda–Navan line, which alternative route to Navan used part of the 39½-mile Oldcastle branch, opened throughout by March 1863. Passenger services on the Oldcastle branch ceased in April 1958, and freight between Navan and Oldcastle in March 1961. A short section to the Tara zinc mines, west of Navan, reopened in June 1977, and the Navan–Drogheda section remains open for this traffic. Freight on the Navan–Kingscourt section ceased in October 2001. In 2006 the track was still in place, while the distinctive yellow-brick GNR(I) station at Navan, designed by William Mills, remained in use as a railway freight office.

North Kerry

Opened throughout by December 1880, the 70-mile Limerick–Tralee line was built by three railway companies, all of which were to become part of the GSWR. An interesting feature of the line was the need to reverse all trains at the one-time terminus at Newcastle West. The line closed to passengers in February 1963, the last freight used the route in June 1978, and lifting of the track west of Ballingrane commenced in 1988. Although the station at Newcastle West has been demolished most others remain intact, and 7 miles of trackbed have been converted to form part of the Great Southern Trail footpath. Track on the Limerick–Foynes section lingers on, 'mothballed', should the port of Foynes require rail freight transport in the future, and stations such as Adare remain as when the last train left, awaiting the return of trains.

Below left: Ex-GSWR 'J15'-class 0-6-0 No 186, dating from 1879 and preserved by the RPSI, at Lixnaw with an RPSI special from Limerick to Tralee on 3 June 1972. Note the bi-directional signal. The station had closed to passengers in 1963 and the line would close to all traffic in 1977, but Lixnaw station house survives, as does the adjoining Railway Bar. *T. Stephens*

Right: 186 coasts through Partickswell station on the last leg of its journey from Tralee to Limerick with the returning RPSI special on 4 June 1972. The ex-GSWR line on the left is the truncated remains of the Croom branch, which closed completely in March 1967. The line to Foynes runs through this station and is currently 'mothballed' for possible future freight use. *T. Stephens*

Limerick and Sligo

The straggling Limerick–Sligo route was open by October 1895 but is currently closed except for the Sligo–Collooney and Limerick–Ennis sections, the latter having reopened in 1988. The Claremorris–Collooney Junction section, which linked with the SLNCR south of Sligo, closed to passengers in June 1963 and to freight in November 1975. The rest of the line closed to passengers in April 1976, and freight movements ended in 2001, prior to which the route was used by a number of special trains. The 114 miles of closed route is 'mothballed' pending phased reopening from Ennis to Claremorris as part of the proposed Western Rail Corridor.

Right: Ex-GSWR 'J15' 0-6-0 No 184, dating from 1880, traverses the old GSWR line between Athenry and Craughwell in May 1982. This was before the Limerick–Sligo line north of Ennis was taken out of use (in 2002), except for the occasional weed-killing train. The route forms part of the proposed Western Rail Corridor, which would see the line reopened. *J. Whiteley*

18 Are ye right there, Michael?

The West Clare Railway was built under the 1883 Light Railways Act and ran some 27 miles from Ennis to Milltown Malbay. The South Clare Railway continued the route on to Kilkee and constructed a branch to Kilrush. Altogether a 53-mile narrow-gauge network was operating for passengers by August 1892.

The railway was renowned because of the music-hall song by Percy French, and the following extracts give a flavour of the song.

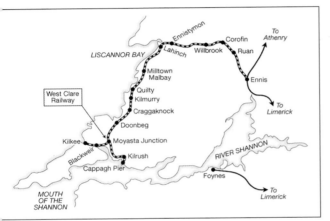

You may talk of Columbus's sailing
Across the Atlantic sea
But he never tried to go railing
From Ennis as far as Kilkee.

They find out where the engine's been hiding,
And it drags you to sweet Corofin;
Says the guard: 'Back her down on the siding,
There's the goods from Kilrush comin' in.'

At Lahinch the sea shines like a jewel,
With joy you are ready to shout,
When the stoker cries out: 'There's no fuel,
And the fire is taytotallay out.'

Kilkee? Oh you never get near it!
You're in luck if the train brings you back,
For the permanent way is so queer, it
Spends most of its time off the track.

Uphill the ould engine is climbin'
While the passengers push with a will;
You are in luck when you reach Ennistymon,
For all the way home is downhill.

And as you're wobbling through the dark,
You hear the guard make this remark:
'Are ye right there, Michael? Are ye right?
Do ye think that ye'll be home before it is light?

The song originated from an unfortunate experience that Percy French, the Irish poet and entertainer, had on the West Clare line. He had intended to provide a show at Kilkee, but his train broke down and he arrived at Kilkee some 5 hours late, by which time his audience had gone home. He sued the railway for loss of earnings and won his case. The negative tone of the song did little for the West Clare Railway's reputation, and there were some that blamed the verse for the line's demise, even though the incident occurred in 1898.

The mile-long Kilrush–Cappagh Pier section, where ships once provided a connection to Limerick, closed to regular traffic in 1916. Rumours of closure of the rest of the line first began circulating in 1945, but plans to convert the route to the Irish standard gauge were considered. Although these plans were not proceeded with, on the grounds of cost, four new diesel railcars were purchased in 1952, and three diesel locomotives took over all freight in 1955. The number of passenger trains, speeds and traffic all increased, but in 1958 the calls for closure returned. A reprieve was granted while roads were improved, but by this time the West Clare was the only CIE narrow-gauge passenger line remaining, and unfortunately was seen as an anachronism. Closure was planned for the end of 1960, but opposition brought a stay of execution to 31 January 1961, by which time it was the last surviving narrow-gauge passenger line in the whole of Ireland. Moyasta Junction is today the centre for the preserved West Clare Railway.

ENNIS, MILTOWN MALBAY, KILRUSH, and KILKEE.—West Clare.
Man., P. Sullivan, Ennis.

Miles	Down.	Week Days.							Sndys		Miles	Up.	Week Days.					Sndys	
		mrn	mrn	non	aft	aft			mrn	aft			mrn	mrn	aft	aft	aft	mrn	aft
	Ennis ....dep.	5 0	8 30	12 0		6 20			5 0		2¼	Kilkee ......dep.	7 25	11 15	2 5	5 30	8 35	7 25	5 30
6¼	Ruan............	Sig.	Sig.	Sig.		Sig.			Sig.		5	Blackweir.......	Sig.	Sig.	Sig.	Sig.	Sig.	Sig.	
8¼	Corofin.........	5 25	9 5	1225		6 45			5 25			Moyasta Junc.arr.	7 40	11 30	2 20	5 45	8 55	7 45	5 45
12	Willbrook.......	Sig.	Sig.	Sig.		Sig.			Sig.		9	Kilrush. {arr.	8 0	12 0	3 0		9 15	8 0	
18¼	Ennistymon....	6 5	9 50	1 5		7 25			6 5			Kilrush. {dep.	7 30	11 20	2 10	5 35			5 35
20¼	Lehinch........	6 15	10 0	1 15		7 35			6 15			Moyasta Junc.dep.	7 50	11 40	2 40	5 55			5 55
27	Miltown Malbay.	6 40	1025	1 40		7 55			6 40		10¼	Doonbeg.......	8 15	1157	3 5	6 13			6 13
31¼	Quilty.........	6 55	1045	Sig.		8 15			6 55		13¼	Craggaknock....	Sig.	Sig.	Sig.	Sig.			Sig.
32¼	Kilmurry........	7 0	1050	2 0		8 20			7 0		15¼	Kilmurry........	8 35	1215	3 30	6 30			6 30
34¼	Craggaknock	Sig.	Sig.	Sig.		Sig.			Sig.		16¼	Quilty..........	8 43	1220	3 37	6 35			6 35
37¼	Doonbeg	7 20	1115	2 20		8 35			7 20		21	Miltown Malbay	9 10	1240	4 0	6 55			6 55
43	Moyasta Junc.arr.	7 40	1140	2 40		8 55			7 40		27¼	Lehinch........	9 35	1 0	4 25	7 15			7 15
47	Kilrush {arr.	8 0	12 0	3 0		9 15			8 0		29¼	Ennistymon.....	9 55	1 10	4 40	7 25			7 25
	Kilrush {dep.	7 30	1120	2 10	5 35					5 35	36	Willbrook......	Sig.	Sig.	Sig.	Sig.			Sig.
—	Moyasta Junc.dep.	7 45	1145	2 45	5 55	9 0			7 45	5 55	39¼	Corofin.........	1030	1 45	5 15	7 55			7 55
45¼	Blackweir.......	Sig.	Sig.	Sig.	Sig.	Sig.			Sig.	Sig.	41¼	Ruan...........	Sig.	Sig.	Sig.	Sig.			Sig.
48	Kilkee ......arr.	8 0	12 0	3 0	6 15	9 15			8 0	6 15	48	Ennis 899....arr.	1055	2 15	5 50	8 20			8 20

Above: Ennis–Kilrush–Kilkee timetable, April 1910.

Left: Prior to replacement by diesels (in 1955) No 5 *Slieve Callan*, an 0-6-2T built by Dübs in 1892, leaves Moyasta Junction heading northwards to Ennis. The leading coach was one of several six-wheeled saloons with large windows built for tourist traffic. The locomotive has been preserved, while Moyasta Junction is now the centre for the restored section of the West Clare Railway. *Ian Allan Library*

Right: 'At Lahinch the sea shines like a jewel'; this was where the West Clare line met the coast. Seen at the station on 28 June 1955 are 2-6-2T No 2C on a goods train and railcar No 3386 at the platform. Slate from Lahinch to Cappagh Pier was one of the many sources of freight traffic for the railway, which at its peak owned more than 1,500 wagons. No 2C, dating from 1900, would be scrapped shortly after this photograph was taken. *P. Gray*

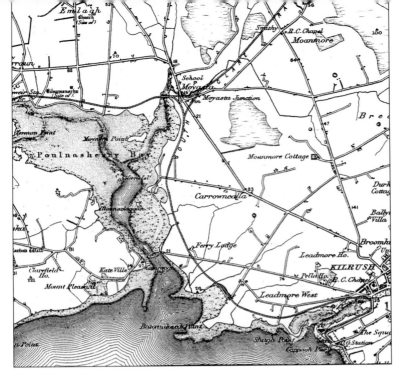

Left: Map of the Moyasta Junction–Kilrush line in 1901. *based on Ordnance Survey Ireland Permit No 8018, © Ordnance Survey Ireland and Government of Ireland*

Right: In 1955 three diesel locomotives were introduced, to replace steam altogether. Here one of the centre-cab locomotives built in Wigan by Walker Bros heads a passenger train at Asylum Gates level crossing, near Lifford; note the three-lever ground frame in the foreground. All the line's diesels would be scrapped after closure of the railway in 1961. *D. Lawrence*

Left: A railcar and van for Kilrush at the Kilrush platform at Moyasta Junction in 1957. Ennis–Kilrush through trains were met here by connections for Kilkee, while the triangular platform arrangement was also used to turn the uni-directional railcars. *D. Lawrence*

Above: 'Kilkee? Oh you never get near it!' Kilkee station on 7 June 1954, with a railcar at the platform and goods stock in the sidings (left). The railcars could reach speeds of up to 35mph and provided hope for the retention of the line; it was rumoured upon closure that these relatively new cars would be sold to the Isle of Man Railway, but this proved unfounded. The station, with its distinctive canopy, survives today as a private residence. *T. Widd*

Centre right: The view at Kilrush station, looking towards Cappagh Pier, on 17 July 1957. A railcar trailer, converted from steam-hauled stock, and a luggage van form the 4.45pm service over the wild and meandering route to Ennis. The line to Cappagh Pier had fallen out of regular use in the 1920s, but the track would remain until closure of the entire system. All the buildings seen here remained in 2006. *C. Boocock*

Right: Forming the 11am service from Ennis, West Clare railcar No 3387 calls at Lahinch station on a windswept 31 January 1961. This was the very last day of operation of the West Clare line and the end of the narrow-gauge era in Ireland. It was a sad day, but the West Clare line lives on, both in its preserved section at Moyasta Junction and in Irish folklore. *N. McAdams*

19 Double-headed from Dingle

The Tralee & Dingle Railway opened in April 1891 and was constructed under the terms of the Light Railways Act of 1883. The 3ft-gauge railway ran for some 31½ miles from Tralee across the Dingle Peninsula to the fishing port of Dingle, while a 6-mile branch ran to Castlegregory. A picturesque line, it passed through a mountainous area in its central section resulting in steep gradients, a horseshoe bend and viaduct. The Dingle Peninsula is one of the more remote areas of Ireland, but the spectacular scenery led to early tourism.

At Tralee a tramway section through the town connected with the GSWR freight-transfer yard, and a flag-waving guard preceded trains as they ran through the streets. South of Tralee there were a number of gated road crossings close to the River Lee, which on occasions flooded the track; the line then largely followed the road to Castlegregory Junction. Beyond here was the famous bank at Glenagalt, the longest and steepest gradient in Ireland, which climbed to 680ft in less than 4 miles at a continuous gradient of 1 in 30/31. The descent into Dingle led onto the pier, the most westerly narrow-gauge railhead in Europe.

Decline set in after World War 1, and the line was absorbed into the GSR. The area served was sparsely populated and two daily passenger trains sufficed, taking about 2½ hours from Dingle to Tralee. The line closed to passengers in April 1939, due partly to the state of the track, which would have needed extensive re-laying to enable passenger services to continue. The Castlegregory branch closed completely at this time, but the main line continued to see regular freight trains until 1947. Thereafter the railway clung on to life thanks to monthly cattle trains, which operated in connection with the famous Dingle Cattle Fair. The numbers of cattle being sent to greener pastures, particularly in the autumn, could not be met by road transport alone, and this enabled the railway to continue in operation, with the remaining locomotives double-heading trains loaded to a maximum of 17 decrepit grey cattle trucks and a brake van. Minimal maintenance of the rusting and overgrown track, mountain mists or rain resulting in slippery rails, heavily loaded trains and steep gradients required valiant efforts by the crews to prevent stalling on the grades. However, these difficulties, combined with the beauty of the area, conspired to make watching such trains a truly enthralling experience.

Although the railway had never been profitable, such limited use could not be justified, and the line was lifted after the final cattle special in June 1953. Locomotive No 5T, shipped to the USA after use on the CLR, later returned home and now runs on the preserved Tralee–Blennerville section of the TDR line.

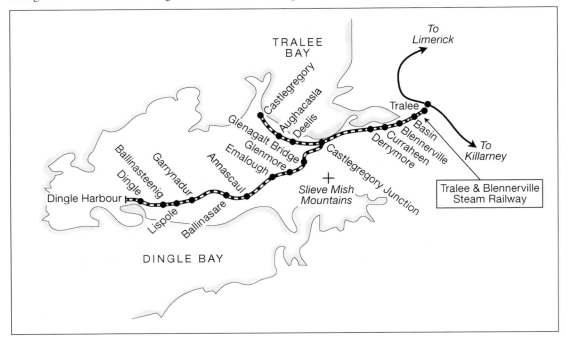

Right: 2-6-0T No 1T, dating from 1889, approaches Ashe Street in Tralee on 24 August 1951, using the roadside line after coaling at the standard-gauge yard. The suffix 'T', denoting the Tralee & Dingle section, was added to all locomotive numbers when the line was taken over by the GSR. The building behind the locomotive was one of the few from its period to survive in this part of Tralee in 2005. *Ian Allan Library*

Below: A cattle special, headed by 2-6-0Ts Nos 8T and 2T, in difficulties on the steep gradient near Puck Island on Saturday 25 August 1951. The need for powerful locomotives on the steep central section of the line is readily apparent. *Ian Allan Library*

Below: 2-6-0Ts Nos 1T and 2T in charge of the monthly Dingle–Tralee cattle train in July 1951. The railway had more than 30 cattle wagons, and in summer the specials ran out to Dingle on the last Friday of the month to serve Dingle Cattle Fair, returning the following day. Dating from 1898, the locomotives seen here would both be scrapped in 1953. *P. Whitehouse*

Below: No 2T, a Hunslet-built 2-6-0T dating from 1889, being hand-turned at Dingle on 24 August 1951. By this time the one-time TDR had become a fascinating part of CIE, attracting many railway enthusiasts keen to catch a last glimpse of the line in operation. The locomotive would be scrapped two years later, upon closure of the line. *Ian Allan Library*

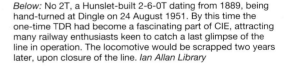

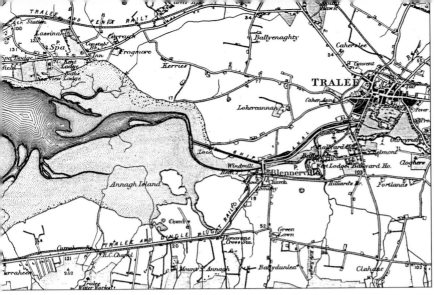

Left: Map of railways in the Tralee Bay area in 1910. *based on Ordnance Survey Ireland Permit No 8018, © Ordnance Survey Ireland and Government of Ireland*

Centre left: Dingle's stone engine shed dated from 1914 and was the most westerly in Europe. It is seen here, together with the water tower, with 2-6-0T No 8T in steam after the cessation of regular services, excepting the monthly cattle specials. Before the line closed entirely most locomotives had been transferred to other narrow-gauge lines, leaving only two fully serviceable on the TDR. *Ian Allan Library*

Below left: Dingle station's overall roof, which was replaced after the original had been destroyed during 'The Troubles', remained after track removal following departure of the last train on 27 June 1953. When this photograph was taken some years later the station was still being used as a road-haulage depot. *D. Lawrence*

Below : Unlike the engine shed the water tower at Dingle survived on 25 May 2005, when this view was recorded. The main station buildings also survive, albeit in a rather modified form, used by a firm of undertakers. *Author*

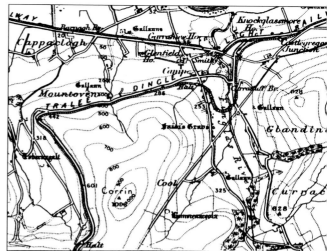

Above: The central girders of Lispole Viaduct, seen here in August 2005, proved to be a bit weak, and trains were limited to 2½mph over this section. Double-headed trains were required to split, each locomotive proceeding separately over the bridge — a practice that in later years was not always strictly observed. *Author*

Above right: Map of the Curraduff Viaduct diversion and Glenagalt Bank in 1910. *based on Ordnance Survey Ireland Permit No 8018, © Ordnance Survey Ireland and Government of Ireland*

Centre right: In less than 4 miles the line climbed from almost sea level at Castlegregory Junction to 680ft at the summit of Glenagalt Bank, providing breathtaking views of Tralee Bay below. Near the summit it was crossed by two bridges, one carrying a farm track and one giving access to a small quarry; both survive, the former being seen here on 25 May 2005. Note that Glenagalt is nowadays spelled as 'Glounagalt'. *Author*

Below right: Seen here on 25 May 2005, the original Curraduff Viaduct, with a 3-chain-radius curve and on a rising gradient, was superseded by a new structure on a different alignment, opened in 1908. This was prompted by an accident in May 1893 whereby a runaway train from Dingle had crashed 50ft from the viaduct into the river below, with the loss of three crew and some 80 pigs; fortunately the passenger carriage of the mixed train did not fall from the viaduct. The new Curraduff Viaduct was of conventional girder construction and also survives. *Author*

Below: The substantial water tower at Castlegregory Junction endures, as do the nearby Railway and Junction bars. A plaque on the water tower records the site of the former junction, which was situated at the base of the infamous Glenagalt Bank. Driving on the nearby road gives an indication of how steep this bank was, as in no time the line and road are high above the shoreline and Castlegregory. *Author*

TRALEE & DINGLE
LIGHT RAILWAY
1891 - 1953
THIS IS THE SITE OF
CASTLEGREGORY JUNCTION

20 Kerry contrasts

Two lines in County Kerry could not have presented more of a contrast: one was specifically designed to be lightly constructed, while the other involved massive engineering works.

The one-line railway

Ballybunion was once connected to the North Kerry line by the Listowel & Ballybunion Railway. Plans for a conventional narrow-gauge line were discarded in favour of a unique 9¼-mile monorail, which was promoted as cheap to build and requiring less land than would a conventional railway. The system used was invented by a Frenchman, Charles Lartigue, built by a German engineer, and opened, in March 1888, by an English company. The carriages and the twin-boiler Mallet-designed locomotives straddled the single rail, which was supported 3ft 3in from the ground on 'A'-frame trestles. Changing from one line to another, level crossings and goods vehicles all presented unique problems. Mobile steps were provided on the train to enable passengers to cross over the elevated rail, while heavy loads had to be balanced on each side.

Although the system worked, the ride quality left something to be desired, and on a few occasions Third-class passengers were obliged to help push the train up the gradient to Ballybunion. In spite of this the railway attracted international attention — there was simply no passenger line like it anywhere. Yet it did not survive

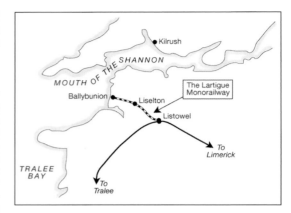

damage in 'The Troubles' and was closed in October 1924 when the GSR refused to have anything to do with it. However, a section of the unique monorail has been recreated at Listowel and is becoming a deserved tourist attraction.

Below: One of the 0-3-0 Hunslet-built double engines at Ballybunion station, giving an indication of the uniqueness of the line. The 10-ton engines were capable of hauling 140 tons on the level. Maximum speed was 20mph, but all the indications are that the journey was noisy, with rumblings, screeching and unnerving pitching. *Ian Allan Library*

Right: The original corrugated-iron waiting room at Listowel in May 2005, more than 80 years after closure. This structure was in sharp contrast to the neighbouring and imposing stone-built GSWR main-line station, which building also survives. *Author*

Right: Map of Ballybunion in 1901. The line continued beyond the passenger station to sand pits; the sand was mixed with seaweed and used to improve the fertility of farmland. *based on Ordnance Survey Ireland Permit No 8018,* © *Ordnance Survey Ireland and Government of Ireland*

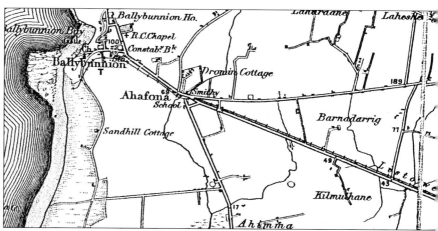

Left: The foundations of one of the monorail turntables at Listowel in May 2005. Turnaround manœuvres for locomotives at each end of the line were complex compared to those on a conventional railway, but up to five connections could be made from the turntables, designed by Fritz Behr. The railway, which was damaged during 'The Troubles', was dismantled by a Sheffield scrap merchant, and little remained after closure. *Author*

LISTOWEL and BALLYBUNION—(1st and 3rd class). Manager, P. McCarthy.														
Miles	Down	Week Days			Sats.	Sundays		Miles	Up	Week Days			Sundays	
		mrn	aft	aft		aft	mrn aft				mrn	aft	aft	aft	aft
	Listowel .....dep.	8 5	12 40	4 0	4 e 0	4 45	11 10 3 0		Ballybunion .dep.	10 30	2 30	5 45		2 0	6 30
4¼	Liselton	8 25	1 0	4e20		5 5	11 20 3 20	4¼	Liselton	10 50	2 50	6 5		2 20	6 50
9¼	Ballybunion . arr.	8 45	1 20	4e40		5 25	11 50 3 40	9¼	Listowel 8 99 . arr.	11 10	3 10	6 25		2 40	7 10

e Except Saturdays.

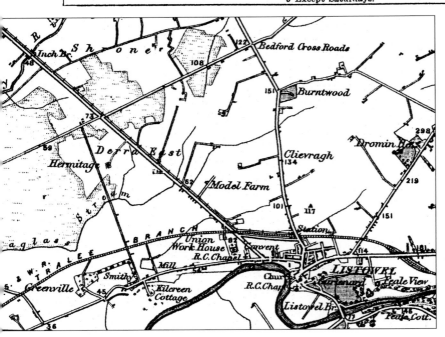

Above: Listowel–Ballybunion timetable, April 1910.

Left: Map of Listowel in 1901, showing the monorail and the North Kerry line. *based on Ordnance Survey Ireland Permit No 8018,* © Ordnance Survey Ireland and Government of Ireland

Left: This former Listowel & Ballybunion Railway bridge at Listowel, photographed in May 2005, is one of two conventional bridges remaining on the line and is located where the railway joined the road, which it followed for much of its route to Ballybunion. Where level crossings were provided the track was hinged to turn at right angles, although in some instances a form of drawbridge was also used. *Author*

Above right: GSR 'J15' 0-6-0 No 133, with double smokebox doors, stands at Valencia Harbour (sometimes spelled 'Valentia') on 11 July 1934. The terminus — the most westerly in Europe — was a simple halt and consisted of a corrugated-iron shed and platform. A ferry crossed to Valencia Island itself, the ultimate western extremity of the continent. The station would close in February 1960. *H. C. Casserley*

Right: Farranfore–Valencia Harbour timetable, April 1910.

Viaducts to Valencia

Valencia Harbour was at the end of a 39¼-mile line from Farranfore, but unlike the monorail this was a very substantially built line. The first section, to Killorglin, was opened in 1885 but was extended under financial guarantees from the GSWR in 1893. It served the most westerly railhead in the whole of Europe, at Valencia Harbour, and also passed through some of the most spectacular scenery in Ireland, including the Killarney lakes; at Caragh Lake the railway purchased a hotel. The line then ran high up between the shores of Dingle Bay and the Teermoyle Mountains. Dank tunnels, a stone shelter to protect the line from rock falls, substantial viaducts and romantically named stations, such as Mountain Stage, made the route Ireland's equivalent to Scotland's West Highland line.

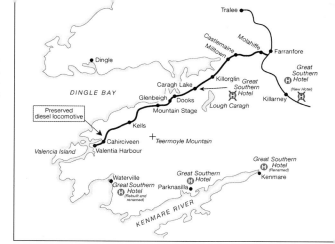

FARRANFORE, KILLORGLIN, KELLS, and VALENCIA HARBOUR.—Great Southern and Western.

Miles	Down.			Week Days.					Miles	Up.			Week Days.			
		mrn	3 cl.	mrn	mrn	aft	aft	aft			mrn	aft	aft	aft		
	Farranfore .... dep.			9 23	11 5	4 0	5 34	....		Valencia Harbour.....dep.	8 20	1 20	4 30	6 5	....	
1¾	Molahiffe			9 27	11 8	4 3	5 38	....	2¾	Cahirciveen, for { arr.	8 25	1 25	4 39	6 10	....	
6¼	Castlemaine			9 37	1118	4 12	5 48	....		Waterville........ { dep.	8 30	1 35	5 10	....	....	
7½	Milltown (Kerry)			9 42	1122	4 16	5 53	....	8¼	Kells........................	8 51	1 58	5 33	....	....	
12¾	Killorglin	6 33	9 53	1132	4 27	6 4	....	15¼	Mountain Stage	9 19	2 26	6 4	....	....	
16	Caragh Lake, for Glencar.	6 45		1142	4 39	....	....	19¾	Glenbeigh	9 34	2 41	6 23	....	....	
18½	Dooks	Sig.		1148	4 45	....	....	21	Dooks	9 39	2 46	6 29	....	....	
19¼	Glenbeigh	6 58		1153	4 50	....	....	23¾	Caragh Lake, for Glencar.	9 46	2 53	6 38	....	....	
23¾	Mountain Stage	7 26		12 7	5 3	5 29		26¾	Killorglin	9 57	3 4	7 10	....	....	
30¼	Kells	7 57		1235	5 30	5 50		31	Milltown (Kerry)	10 6	3 13	7 24	....	....	
36¼	Cahirciveen, for { arr.	8 26		1252	5 50			32¼	Castlemaine	10 10	3 17	7 35	....	....	
	Waterville........ { dep.	7 45	8 30	1255	3 45	5 55		38¼	Molahiffe	10 22	3 29	7 50	....	....	
39¼	Valencia Harbour ....arr.	7 52	8 37	1 0	3 52	6 0		39¼	Farranfore (above)....arr.	10 25	3 32	7 54	....	....	

Mixed trains were run, and the passenger service was sparse. In 1910 the fastest of three passenger services took about two hours. By 1954 the single passenger train took 15 minutes longer, and for a time operating practices enabled some trains to wait at Killorglin, so that passengers could do their shopping. Modern diesels were introduced on the line, albeit hauling ancient rolling-stock, but this was a remote area, and losses mounted. While closure of such a scenic route was met with dismay, it was perhaps surprising that the line should have survived so long. It closed to all traffic in February 1960, although cattle trains ran until August. Being of sturdy construction, many relics are still to be seen, and all the principal viaducts and tunnels on the route survive.

Above: Metropolitan Vickers diesel-electric No C229 and a van stand at the very end of the most westerly line in Europe, at Valencia Harbour. CIE ordered 33 of these 550hp Bo-Bo locomotives for use on secondary lines such as this. *The Rev J. Parker*

Below: A Metro-Vick Bo-Bo (No C227) once used on the line is preserved in original silver livery at Cahirciveen and is seen here in May 2005 masquerading as No C202, which locomotive hauled the last train from Cahirciveen. Unfortunately the static exhibit, which has no engine within, had suffered considerable vandalism, and everything in the cabs that could be broken had been broken. *Author*

Left: Cahirciveen Viaduct, 940ft long, was built in 1893 over the tidal estuary of the River Fertha. Seen here in May 2005, it has been out of use since 1960, although the guide rails for the wooden track supports give the impression that track still runs across it. *Author*

Above: Kells station was close to the summit of the route and was one of a number of passing-places on the single line. The station building, seen here in May 2005, and the nearby signalbox have been preserved to high standards and now provide community facilities. The corrugated-iron station was similar in its design to those at Valencia and Kenmare. The station safe has remained locked since the line closed, the keys having been lost. *Author*

Below: Drivers'-eye view of Cahirciveen Viaduct, looking towards Kells, from the windowless cab of the preserved diesel in May 2005. The journey time for the 6¼-mile Cahirciveen–Kells section was no less than half an hour. *Author's collection*

Left: The stone portal of Drung Hill No 1 Tunnel, seen in May 2005. The 120yd tunnel was one of two, almost adjoining, that cut through outcrops of the Teermoyle Mountains; at this point the route was cut high in the mountainside and afforded stunning panoramic views of Dingle Bay. The line was the first to use the electric train-staff system; note the insulators for wires that once ran along the crown of the tunnel. *Author*

Below: Standing high above the river from which it takes its name, Laune Viaduct is of a bowstring girder design comprising three 105ft spans. Located just to the east of the stone-built Killorglin station, which survives as a private residence, the rusting structure was in use as a footpath when photographed in May 2005. *Author*

Left: Gleensk Viaduct, dating from 1893 and seen here in May 2005, is one of the most impressive disused viaducts in Ireland and remains open to walkers. At its highest the curving steel-and-stone structure stands 73ft above the river level, while the 11 spans are on a radius of 10 chains, necessitating a check rail. *Author*

21 The fate of freight

The limited nature of mineral deposits in Ireland constrained industrialisation and meant that rail freight was never as heavy as in many parts of Britain. Yet agricultural traffic — livestock in particular — was once significant, cattle trains being a distinctive feature of the Irish rail scene. Such was the scale of cattle traffic that freight locomotives were often referred to as 'cattle engines'. The monthly cattle fairs kept lines and stations alive with frantic peaks of activity, and for the very largest livestock fairs as many as 50 extra trains might be run in the space of a week.

Irish cattle wagons were distinctive in that many had no roof and that bulls and heifers were kept separate, but rules limiting wagons to specific numbers of cattle and stipulating the laying down of straw for breeding cattle were not always strictly observed. The welfare of some animals left much to be desired, and cattle were sometimes knocked about by shunting operations and in trans-shipment during their journey. As late as the 1960s long trains of cattle wagons could still be seen wending their way to ports for export, but all livestock trains had ceased running by 1975. Other agricultural freight was also conveyed by rail. Potatoes were important, and sugar beet was carried until 2006.

Mixed freight and passenger trains were once a regular feature on most lines, while dock traffic, at Dublin and Belfast in particular, was at one time extensive. In 1966 the UTA won a contract to carry more than 4 million tons of spoil for a road project, some 7,500 spoil trains being run until 1970, but otherwise, Belfast and Londonderry excepted, the UTA ceased carrying freight on its surviving lines.

In the Republic some lines that closed to passengers remained open for freight for many years, often with ever-deteriorating track. Nonetheless, many freight-only lines are now closed, including, in recent times, the Limerick–Claremorris and Kingscourt–Navan lines.

There has also been a decline in freight movements. By way of example, in 1999 timber accounted for 15 trains a week, but by 2002 this had reduced to four trains, although pulpwood traffic continues. In 2001 the closure of Irish Fertiliser Industries meant the loss of the railways' largest freight customer.

Containers were introduced by the pre-Grouping companies and expanded by CIE in 1969. The original containers could be transferred to narrow-gauge lines. Today's container trains have also been cut back, and in 2004 services to Mallow, Tralee, Sligo and Longford were withdrawn.

Currently there is no significant freight activity in Northern Ireland, while in the Republic there has been little investment in freight since the 1970s. However, while there has been some consolidation, some worthwhile flows remain. Furthermore, a number of unused lines have been retained to allow for potential new rail freight in the future.

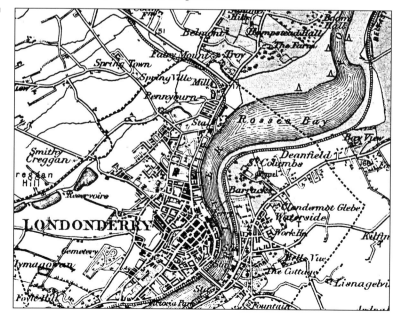

Right: Map of the four lines into Londonderry in 1902. *Crown copyright*

Above: A considerable proportion of Ireland's freight was once transported by narrow-gauge trains, and freight services were frequently mixed with passenger. Here, on 14 June 1957, CLR No 12L, a 2-4-2T originally from the Cork, Blackrock & Passage Railway, is seen shunting a long train of covered vans at the Dromod transfer sidings, shared with the MGWR. The overgrown cattle stalls can be seen on the left of the picture. *L. Nicolson*

Left: Mixed-gauge track and a turntable can be seen on the lower deck of Craigavon Bridge, over the River Foyle at Londonderry, on 18 April 1948. The Londonderry Port & Harbour Commissioners ran a mixed-gauge railway on the bridge, which provided a link between the four separate rail lines serving Londonderry. Capstans were used to move wagons across the bridge, locomotives not being permitted on account of a weight restriction. The line would close in August 1962. *H. C. Casserley*

Left: A train of CIE and ex-GNR(I) covered wagons forming the 2.50pm Portadown–Omagh goods, hauled by UTA ex-GNR(I) 0-6-0 No 33, heads out of Pomeroy on 25 July 1964. Freight was once so heavy that goods trains ran at night so as not to disrupt passenger services. The line was to close the following year, all remaining freight traffic being transferred by the UTA onto the area's roads. *E. Patterson*

Above: The daily goods at Castlecomer on 28 August 1957. The branch was normally worked by the Kilkenny pilot but on this occasion had been substituted by 'J15' 0-6-0 No 164. In the foreground is the beginning of the extension to Deerpark Colliery, which opened in 1920. The branch would close in 1963. Before road haulage took hold the railways distributed most coal supplies in Ireland, including considerable imported supplies. *A. Donaldson*

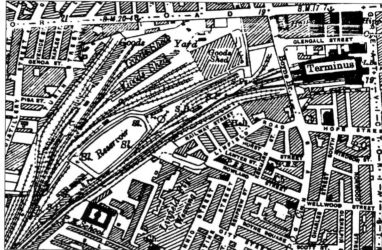

Right: Map of the Grosvenor Road goods yard in central Belfast in 1938. The depot closed in 1965, and some buildings were demolished, but many remain. The area has since become the Grosvenor Road Business Park. *Crown copyright*

Right: Irish agriculture was at one time largely rail-orientated, and the cattle train was a distinctive feature of Irish freight operations. In 1900 some 2.3 million animals, including pigs and sheep, were conveyed by rail, earning the railways more income than any other freight. Cattle were the most important, and some can be seen here being loaded at Tralee in August 1974. Tralee freight yard was disused by 2005. *M. Baker*

Above Left: Small and light 150hp 0-4-0 diesel-hydraulic locomotive No G603 at Ferbane with a Clara–Banagher freight on 11 October 1958. Although the innovative use of such motive power cut costs and track maintenance the 18¼-mile ex-GSWR line would close to freight in January 1963. *C. Fry*

Left: CIE Metropolitan-Vickers/GM Co-Co diesel-electric No 005 passes Wilkinson station gates with a Kingscourt–Drogheda freight on 17 June 1976. Flows of gypsum to Dublin North Wall would continue until 31 October 2001. *A. Dale*

Above: General Motors-built Bo-Bo diesel-electric No 185 heads a train of palletised bagged cement, destined for Sligo, at Longford freight terminal. Bulk cement was still carried by rail in 2006, but the wide range of freight that once used Irish lines is now greatly reduced. The terminal seen here closed in 2004. *D. Carse*

Right: The ex-MGWR Navan–Kingscourt line closed to passengers in 1947, although freight continued until October 2001. The track, increasingly covered with vegetation, remained when this view, looking north towards Proudstown Park, was recorded just outside Navan in August 2003. A goods office continued to make use of the former GNR(I) passenger station at Navan, in connection with the remaining Tara Mines–Drogheda freight link. *Author*

Left: More overgrown track, on the Waterford–New Ross line, in August 2005. Regular freight ended in September 1976, and all services in January 1995. Rails have been removed on the northern section of this ex-Dublin & South Eastern Railway branch, but the track still remains on a short southern section. *Author*

Right: Tankers once used to carry molasses, seen abandoned at Foynes in May 2005. Since closure to freight in December 2001 the entire ex-GSWR Limerick–Foynes line has been 'mothballed' for potential future use. The retention of track represents a sensible and farsighted course of action for the future of rail freight. *Author*

Below: A complicated junction on the Bord na Móna bog railway system; note the logs pushed under the track to prevent it from sinking into the soft bog land. Although Ireland's last narrow-gauge passenger lines closed early in 1961, several hundred miles of narrow-gauge bog railway remain, track being lifted and re-laid as cutting of the peat progresses. *E. Gilmore*

22 Last calls in County Cork

The Blarney Tram

The Cork & Muskerry Light Railway operated a network of 3ft-gauge lines from its Cork Western Road terminus north-westward to Coachford, Blarney and Donoughmore. The lines were constructed under the provisions of the Light Railways Act of 1883, the first 8¾-mile section, to Blarney, opening in August 1887. The line was extended to Coachford in March of the following year, and a further 9-mile branch to Donoughmore opened in May 1894.

The mainly roadside lines served the exclusive hydro at St Anne's and conveyed tourists to Blarney Castle, where the station was located at the castle gates. The 'Blarney Tram', as it was known, was profitable until World War 1, and the isolated system became part of the GSR in 1925. Bus competition ate into the revenue, and although a temporary halt beside the Cork Exhibition of 1932 provided additional traffic

the network closed in December 1934. After closure one engine was sent to Skibbereen for a while, but none has survived. Little is left of the railway at Cork, although the corrugated-iron station building at Blarney remains.

Right: 4-4-0T No 7 *Peake*, built by the Falcon Engine Co in 1898. During its lifetime the railway operated nine attractive steam locomotives, which were latterly painted in a light-green livery. All would ultimately be scrapped following closure of the line.
Ian Allan Library

Right: The Blarney steam! 4-4-0T No 8 *Dripsey* was the last engine built for the CMLR in 1904. Locomotives were named after locations on the railway, including Blarney, which was the most important tourist destination on the line. Trains from Cork took 37 minutes to reach the station, some 8¾ miles from Cork Western Road.
LPC

Above: A mixed train calls at Carrigrohane station, 3½ miles to the west of Cork Western Road. Although the line used the roadside for much of its route, tramway-style skirts were not fitted to the later locomotives. The attractive location, in a gorge of the River Lee, is still identifiable, albeit rather busier with traffic today. *Ian Allan Library*

Below left: The ex-CMLR station building at Blarney still survived in May 2005, more than 70 years after its closure. Currently used as a shop, it remains in good condition. By any standards this is a remarkable survival at such a prominent location as Blarney Castle. *Author*

Right: CMLR timetable, April 1910.

CORK, BLARNEY, DONOUGHMORE, and COACHFORD (1st and 3rd class)—Cork and Muskerry.
Gen. Man., T. O'Connor, Cork.

(Timetable — Down and Up services, Week Days and Sundays)

† Western Road. ‡ Over 1 mile to G. S. & W. Station. 🚂 All Trains stop at Gurth by Signal.

a Trains stop only by Signal, or on notice being given to the Guard.

Over Roaringwater Bay

Built under the terms of the 1883 Light Railways Act, the 3ft-gauge Schull & Skibbereen Light Railway ran some 15 miles between the port of Schull and the main line at Skibbereen. It opened in September 1886 and was extended from outside Schull station on a curving route to Schull Pier in October 1893.

The maximum gradient was a steep 1 in 24 in parts, as the line was built cheaply with sharp curves and light rails. Nonetheless, at Ballydehob it was forced to cross a deep sea inlet at Roaringwater Bay by means of a substantial 12-arch viaduct, which was the main engineering work.

The line followed the roadside for much of its route, and tramway-style skirts were fitted to the first three locomotives. These proved insufficiently powerful to haul traffic over the steep gradients; constant failures meant that after two years the line had to be closed while they were modified, new locomotives being ordered at the same time.

On reopening of the line the situation improved, but this was a remote area of Ireland, and the settlements served by the railway were small. Even at its peak two trains a day in each direction, with extra trains on fair days, were sufficient. A journey over the 15-mile line took some 80 minutes. Only two of the six intermediate stations — at Hollyhill and Ballydehob — had buildings, although all had raised platforms. At Skibbereen the narrow-gauge

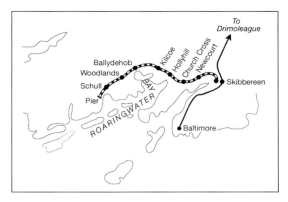

SKIBBEREEN, BALLYDEHOB, and SCHULL (1st and 3rd class).—Schull and Skibbereen.												
		Man., D. Creedon.			Sec., Wm. Goggin.							
Miles	**Down.**		**Week Days.**			Miles	**Up.**			**Week Days.**		
		Except Saturdays and Skibbereen Cattle Fair Days	aft	Saturdays and Skibbereen Cattle Fair Days	aft	aft			Thursdays only	mrn	Mixed Thursdays	mrn	aft
—	Skibbereen . dep.		1230		1 30	6 40	—	Schull ....dep.		7 0		9 30	4 10
3	Newcourt		1243		1 43	6 53	2	Woodlands		7 10		9 40	4 20
4	Church Cross....		1248		1 48	6 58	5	Ballydehob		7 30		10 0	4 40
6	Hollyhill		1257		1 57	7 7	8	Kilcoe		7 47		10 17	4 57
7	Kilcoe.......		1 3		2 3	7 13	9	Hollyhill		7 53		10 23	5 3
10	Ballydehob......		1 25		2 25	7 35	11	Church Cross.....		8 2		10 32	5 12
13	Woodlands......		1 40		2 40	7 50	12	Newcourt........		8 7		10 37	5 17
15	Schull .... arr.		1 50		2 50	8 0	15	Skibbereen 901.a.		8 20		10 50	5 30

Extra.—Schull to Skibbereen, on Skibbereen Cattle Fair Days, at 6 mrn., arriving at 7 20 mrn. Skibbereen to Ballydehob and Schull, on Cattle Fair Days, at 6 mrn., arriving at Ballydehob at 6 50 and Schull at 7 20 mrn. Skibbereen to Ballydehob and Schull on Thursdays at 9 30 mrn., returning from Schull at 12 45 aft.

Above: Schull & Skibbereen Light Railway timetable, April 1910.

Left: A mixed train including a First-class compartment awaits departure from Schull in GSR days. The train is headed by No 3S *Kent*, a 4-4-0T Peckett built in 1914. The local council, which financed the line, argued over the names of locomotives depending on the council's political make-up. Although Schull was a terminus a loop round the station ran on to Schull Pier. Regular trains ceased using the pier in the 1930s. *R. Clements*

Left: A mixed train headed by No 3S waits at the platform at Hollyhill station. Hollyhill and Ballydehob were the only intermediate stations with buildings. The roadside nature of the line is apparent from this view, but the locomotive's original tramway-style skirts had been removed by the GSR. *A. Hughes*

Left: No 3S takes water from the wooden-based water tower at Ballydehob in GSR days. This was the main intermediate station on the line, and passengers had time to stretch their legs before the train departed. The usual journey time over the 15-mile line was about 80 minutes; speeds were limited to 15mph, and there was no signalling. *A. Hughes*

Below: A mixed Skibbereen–Schull train headed by No 3S crosses the road outside Skibbereen station, which was the headquarters of the railway. The narrow-gauge buildings, including the carriage shed, are visible on the left, while the main-line station is in the distance. The train will have reversed into a siding before setting out for Schull. *A. Hughes*

Above: Today remains of the railway can still be found, notably the impressive 12-arch stone viaduct over Roaringwater Bay, seen here in May 2005. Some smaller bridges and earthworks also survive, while a seat from one of the railway's coaches has found its way into a bar at Kilcoe. *Author*

Right: Hollyhill station, approximately halfway between Schull and Skibbereen, once boasted a siding and loading ramp. Seen in derelict condition in May 2005, the small concrete station house, once home to a railway employee, had replaced the original building destroyed in 'The Troubles'. *Author*

Below right: At Schull the station house, goods shed, engine shed and stables all survive. The railway helped local farmers earn a better price for their livestock, but passenger traffic was always limited. Nevertheless, the main station house was substantial, as apparent from this view in May 2005. *Author*

station conveniently adjoined the main-line station, but trains were not timed to make connections. Skibbereen, the main station on the line, was where locomotives and rolling-stock were kept. There was a small workshop, but major repairs were carried out at Cork or Limerick, reached via the standard-gauge lines.

In 1925 the line was taken over by the GSR, which closed the Schull Harbour extension in the 1930s. In 1938 a locomotive was imported from the closed Cork & Muskerry Light Railway; at first the coupling heights were found to be incompatible, and even after modifications the engine was too large for some platforms, but it eventually did some work on the line.

Between April 1944 and December 1945 services were suspended as a result of the fuel crisis. They were withdrawn again in January 1947 by CIE, but this time the railway, which had never made a profit, would not see its services restored. The three surviving locomotives were transported to Inchicore Works at Dublin but not scrapped until 1954. Several remains of the railway can still be found, and stretches of the trackbed are used as footpaths.

23 The Bandon and its abandoned branches

What from 1888 became known as the Cork, Bandon & South Coast Railway ran from Cork Albert Quay station westward into rural areas of County Cork, including Bantry and Skibbereen. Construction by the Cork & Bandon Railway started at the Bandon end, and the first few miles eastward to Ballinhassig opened in June 1849. The line was then extended through Gogginshill Tunnel to Cork, this section opening in December 1851. The West Cork Railway then extended the line from Bandon westward to Dunmanway, which line opened in June 1866. Another

company, the Ilen Valley Railway, extended the route to Skibbereen, opening in July 1877. A further extension to Bantry opened in October 1892, and from 1906 passenger trains served steamships that sailed from Bantry Pier to Glengarriff, among other destinations.

The line to Bantry developed as the main line, but a number of branch lines connected with the system. These included the 11-mile Kinsale Junction–Kinsale branch, opened in June 1863, and the 9-mile Clonakilty Junction–Clonakilty branch, opened in

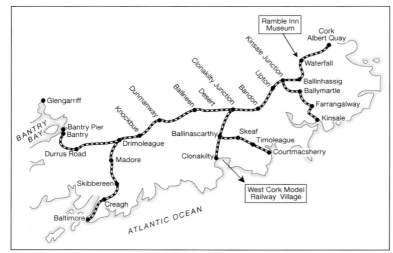

Below: Courtmacsherry was the terminus of the Timoleague & Courtmacsherry Extension Light Railway, opened by 1891. This view, looking towards the pier, features 2-6-0T *Argadeen*, an inside-cylinder Hunslet locomotive built in 1894 and which was to remain in working order until 1957. Note the cowcatcher and bell for roadside running; also the fish vans on the pier and the barefoot boy. The station and line would close in 1961. *LPC*

August 1886, off which branched the 6-mile Ballinascarthy–Timoleague line, opened in December 1890. The last was extended to Courtmacsherry, under the provisions of the Light Railways Acts, by the Timoleague & Courtmacsherry Light Railway, this extension opening in 1891. The branch mainly followed the roadside and was one of the few non-narrow-gauge roadside passenger railways in Ireland. The Skibbereen–Baltimore extension opened in May 1893, Baltimore station being the most southerly in Ireland. At its peak 'The Bandon' operated a network of single and snaking lines covering about 95 miles, although the 9-mile Ballinascarthy–Courtmacsherry branch would remain independent until GSR days.

Initially Albert Quay station was physically separated from the rest of the Irish railway system in Cork, but in 1912 the Cork City Railways provided a link through the city's roads to the rest of the network. Eventually all the lines became part of the GSR, which changed the livery from olive green to grey but introduced some new stock on the route.

The Kinsale branch was the first to close to all traffic, in September 1931. This was followed by passenger services over the short Bantry Town–Bantry Pier section, in September 1937. The Ballinascarthy–Courtmacsherry line closed to passengers in February 1947, although excursions on the line continued until the late 1950s.

Due to the fuel crisis passenger services on all lines were suspended in 1947 for three months, together with Skibbereen–Baltimore freight, but the network continued after this, and diesel railcars were introduced in 1954. However, by this time services had been reduced on the main line to two trains a day in each direction.

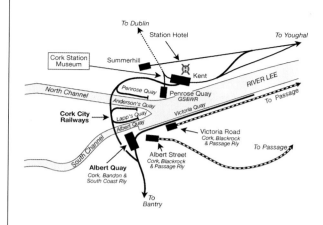

An announcement of the abandonment of all lines was met with dismay in the area, and a campaign, involving local councils and supported by the Church, was mounted to save the remote rural routes. A delegation met with Todd Andrews, then head of CIE, but it was all to no avail, and closure of all remaining lines was effected in April 1961, although the ex-Cork City Railways line continued in use for freight until April 1976. Many remains of the substantially built main line and its abandoned branches can still be found.

Below: The view from a window of an ancient coach on the 10am Cork Albert Quay–Courtmacsherry excursion of Sunday 26 August 1951 as it nears Courtmacsherry. The light railway was planned as as narrow-gauge line but was built to Irish standard gauge. The roadside nature of the extension is apparent from this view. *O. Prosser*

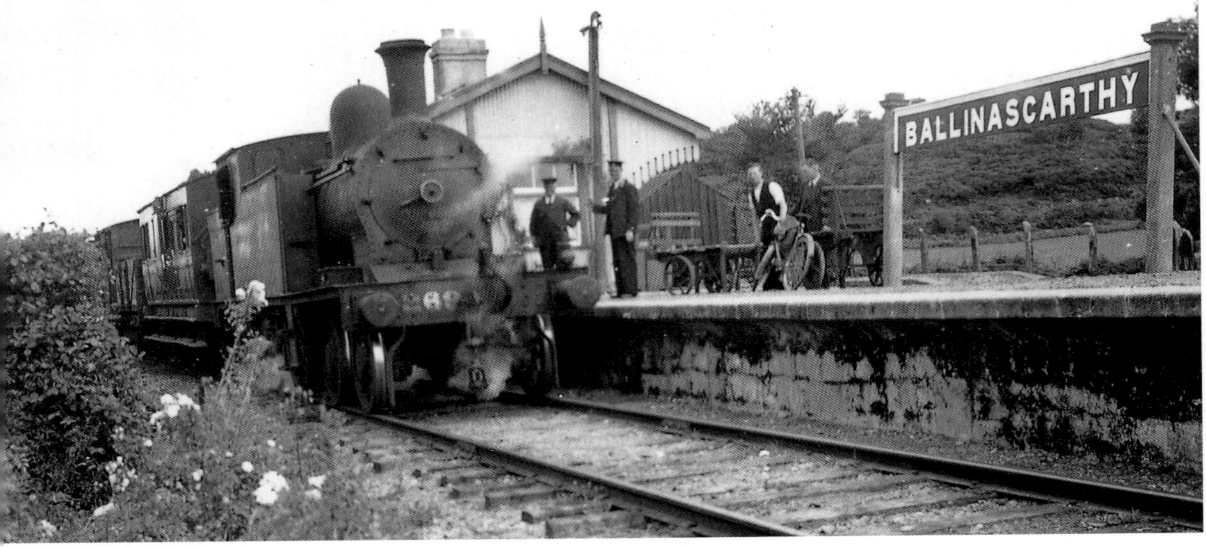

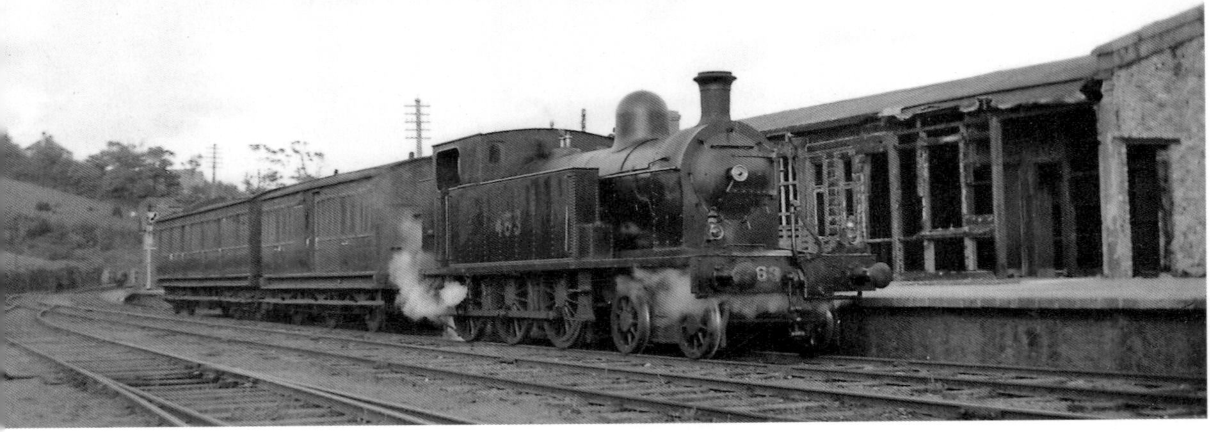

CORK, KINSALE, BANDON, BANTRY, KILLARNEY, and BALTIMORE (1st and 3rd class).—Cork, Bandon, and South Coast.
Offices—Albert Quay, Cork. Gen. Man., John R. Kerr.

Miles	Down.	Week Days. mrn	c	non	c	aft	Sundays. mrn	c	aft	aft
	Albert Quay Station, Cork ....dep.	3 30	9 0	12 0	4 15	5 45	3 30	1030	5 30	
6¼	Waterfall	....	9 17	....	4 32	6 3	....	1047	5 47	
10	Ballinhassig	3 54	9 27	1224	4 41	6 13	3 54	1056	5 57	
13½	Kinsale Junction	....	9 34	1231	4 48	6 22	....	11 4	6 4	
—	Kinsale Junction .dep.	....	9 40	1 45	....	6 25	....	11 6	6 7	9 10
17½	Ballymartle	....	Sig.	Sig.	....	Sig.	....	1118	Sig.	9 22
21¼	Farrangalway	....	10 4	2 9	....	6 50	....	1130	6 31	9 34
24	**Kinsale** ....arr.	....	1013	2 18	....	6 58	....	1139	6 40	9 40
15½	Upton and Innishannon	4 10	9 41	1238	4 55	6 34	4 10	1113	6 11	
20	**Bandon** .... arr.	4 19	9 50	1247	5 4	6 45	4 19	1122	6 22	
	dep.	4 22	9 53	1251	5 6	6 48	4 22	1126	6 25	
24	Clonakilty Junction	....	10 2	1 0	5 15	6 57	....	1135	6 34	
—	Clonakilty Junc...dep.	....	1010	1 8	5 20	6 59	5 50	1137	6 36	
29¼	Ballinascarthy	....	1025	1 23	5 35	7 14	....	1153	6 52	
33	**Clonakilty** ....arr.	....	1037	1 34	....	7 25	6 14	12 4	7 3	
27¾	Desert	....	1013	1 12	5 25	....	....	1147	6 46	
30	Ballineen and Enniskean	4 47	1018	1 17	5 32	....	4 47	1154	6 55	
37¾	Dunmanway	5 3	1033	1 32	5 48	....	5 3	1210	7 13	
42	Knuckbue	....	**d**	....	Sig.	....	....	Sig.	....	
45½	Drimoleague Junc... arr.	5 20	1049	1 48	6 5	....	5 20	1227	7 31	
—	Drimoleague Junc.dep.	5 25	1052	1 51	6 8	....	5 25	1229	....	
52	Durrus Road	....	Sig.	Sig.	Sig.	....	....	Sig.	....	
57¾	**Bantry** ....arr.	6 2	1129	2 27	6 45	....	6 2	1 6	....	
—	*Tourist Car.* **Bantry** ....dep.	....	....	3 15	....	....	....	....	....	
67	Glengarriff... arr.	....	....	5 0	....	....	....	....	....	
	dep.	....	....	....	....	....	....	....	....	
87	Kenmare	....	....	....	....	....	....	....	....	
109	**Killarney** ....arr.	....	....	....	....	....	....	....	....	
—	Drimoleague Junc...dep.	5 26	1053	1 52	6 9	....	5 26	1230	7 36	
49	Madore	....	Sig.	Sig.	Sig.	....	....	Sig.	7 46	
53¾	**Skibbereen 905** .. arr.	5 43	1112	2 9	6 27	....	5 43	1250	7 55	
	dep.	6 30	....	2 12	6 35	....	6 30	2 30	....	
57¾	Creagh	6 40	....	2 22	6 45	....	6 40	2 40	....	
61¾	**Baltimore** ....arr.	6 50	....	2 32	6 55	....	6 50	2 50	....	

Miles	Up.	Week Days. mrn	mrn	mrn	aft	aft	aft	aft	Sundays. mrn	aft	aft
	Baltimore ....dep.	....	8 0	1130	....	....	....	5 45	9 0	....	6 45
4	Creagh	....	8 11	1140	....	....	....	Sig.	9 10	....	Sig.
8	**Skibbereen 905** .. arr.	....	8 20	1150	....	....	....	6 5	9 20	....	7 5
	dep.	....	8 27	1157	....	2 58	....	7 25	9 23	....	7 15
12¾	Madore	....	8 38	Sig.	....	Sig.	....	Sig.	Sig.	....	Sig.
16½	Drimoleague Junc...arr.	....	8 46	1214	....	3 15	....	7 44	9 42	....	7 34
Tourist Car. Mls	**Killarney** .....dep.	....	....	....	....	....	....	....	....	....	....
22	Kenmare	....	....	....	....	....	....	....	....	....	....
42	Glengarriff .. arr.	....	....	....	....	....	....	....	....	....	....
	dep.	....	....	9 30	....	....	....	....	....	....	....
51½	**Bantry** ....arr.	....	**c**	1115	....	**c**	....	....	**c**	....	....
—	— **Bantry** ....dep.	....	8 10	1144	....	2 40	....	7 10	9 8	....	7 0
—	57 Durrus Road	....	8 26	Sig.	....	Sig.	....	Sig.	Sig.	....	7 16
—	63½ Drimoleague Jun. ar.	....	8 42	1215	....	3 14	....	7 42	9 40	....	7 32
—	Drimoleague Junc..dep.	....	8 50	1217	....	3 24	....	7 47	9 45	....	7 39
19¾	Knuckbue	....	Sig.	....	....	**n**	....	....	Sig.	....	....
24	Dunmanway	....	9 8	1234	....	3 43	....	8 4	10 3	....	7 58
31½	Ballineen and Enniskean	....	9 25	1249	....	4 2	....	8 22	1020	....	8 16
34	Desert	....	9 31	1255	....	4 8	....	....	1026	....	8 22
—	Mls **Clonakilty** ......dep.	8 30	....	1235	3 10	....	7 50	....	10 5	....	7 50
—	3¾ Ballinascarthy	8 43	....	1246	3 22	4 0	8 1	....	1016	....	8 1
—	9 Clonakilty Junc. arr.	8 57	....	1 0	3 36	4 17	8 15	....	1031	....	8 15
37¾	Clonakilty Junction	8 58	9 40	1 5	3 37	4 18	8 16	....	1035	....	8 31
41½	**Bandon** .... arr.	9 7	9 49	1 14	3 46	4 27	8 25	8 45	1044	....	8 40
	dep.	9 14	9 51	1 17	3 48	4 32	....	8 48	1047	....	8 44
46½	Upton and Innishannon	9 26	10 1	1 27	3 59	4 42	....	8 58	1057	....	8 54
—	Mls **Kinsale** ....dep.	8 55	....	1 0	3 30	....	....	....	1025	5 20	8 25
—	2¾ Farrangalway	9 4	....	Sig.	3 39	....	....	....	1034	5 29	8 34
—	6¾ Ballymartle	Sig.	....	Sig.	Sig.	....	....	....	1046	5 41	8 46
—	10½ Kinsale Junc. ..arr.	9 27	....	1 30	4 2	....	....	....	1057	5 52	8 57
48¼	Kinsale Junction	9 37	**g**	1 33	4 9	4 49	....	....	11 5	....	9 2
51½	Ballinhassig	9 49	1016	1 42	4 19	**g**	....	9 14	1115	....	9 11
55½	Waterfall	10 1	**g**	....	4 32	**g**	....	....	1124	....	9 21
61¾	Cork † **897**, 902 ..arr.	1015	1040	2 3	4 48	5 23	....	9 35	1140	....	9 35

c Stop at **Aughaville** if required. **d** Stops on Skibbereen, Dunmanway, and Bantry Market Days. **g** Stop to set down from West of Bandon.
n Stops on Skibbereen and Bantry Market Days. † Albert Quay.

Above left: The 10.30am Clonakilty Junction–Clonakilty train waits at Ballinascarthy station on 16 August 1949. After shunting in the sidings adjoining the Ballinascarthy & Timoleague Light Railway the driver, guided by the photographer's hand signals, has set back to this position. Locomotive No 269, a 'G6' 4-4-2T of Robinson design, dated from 1896 and was built for the Waterford, Limerick & Western Railway. It would be out of use by 1957. *O. Prosser*

Left: Ex-Cork, Bandon & South Coast Railway 'B4' 4-6-0T No 463 heads a two-coach train from Cork at Bantry Town on 20 May 1954. Beautiful as this remote area was, it was unable to support sufficient railway patronage, and the line closed in April 1961. The site of the station is now a car park, but one surviving stone building, with heavy iron girders that once supported the water tank, remained in 2005. *C. Cann*

Above: For secondary and branch-line duties CIE ordered a batch of 33 Metropolitan-Vickers Bo-Bo diesel-electric locomotives, fitted with 550hp eight-cylinder Crossley engines. Approaching Timoleague, one of these modern diesels, No C220, heads a motley collection of coaches forming a summer excursion train from Courtmacsherry before final closure of the branch in April 1961. *N. McAdams*

Left: Cork, Kinsale, Bantry and Baltimore timetable, April 1910. Note the 'tourist car' links.

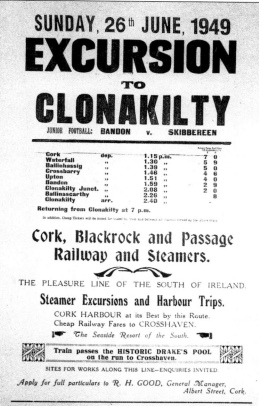

SUNDAY, 26th JUNE, 1949

EXCURSION

TO

CLONAKILTY

JUNIOR FOOTBALL: BANDON v. SKIBBEREEN

				Return Fares 2nd Class TO CLONAKILTY	
Cork	dep.	1.15 p.m.		7	0
Waterfall	,,	1.30	,,	5	9
Ballinhassig	,,	1.39	,,	5	0
Crossbarry	,,	1.46	,,	4	6
Upton	,,	1.51	,,	4	0
Bandon	,,	1.59	,,	2	9
Clonakilty Junct.	,,	2.08	,,	2	0
Ballinascarthy	,,	2.26	,,		8
Clonakilty	arr.	2.40	,,		

Returning from Clonakilty at 7 p.m.

In addition, Cheap Tickets will be issued for travel to, from and between all stations served by the above train.

Cork, Blackrock and Passage Railway and Steamers.

THE PLEASURE LINE OF THE SOUTH OF IRELAND.

Steamer Excursions and Harbour Trips.

CORK HARBOUR at its Best by this Route.
Cheap Railway Fares to CROSSHAVEN.

The Seaside Resort of the South.

Train passes the HISTORIC DRAKE'S POOL
on the run to Crosshaven.

SITES FOR WORKS ALONG THIS LINE—ENQUIRIES INVITED.

Apply for full particulars to R. H. GOOD, *General Manager,*
Albert Street, Cork.

CLONAKILTY JUNCTION
CHANGE HERE FOR CLONAKILTY &
COURTMACSHERRY BRANCH

Left: Metro-Vick/Crossley diesel-electric No C202 heads a mixed train at Skibbereen. The photograph was taken shortly before the end of services on the line, and although some stations were repainted before closure, the external appearance of this locomotive is rather shabby. *D. Lawrence*

Left: A railcar forms a service to Cork Albert Quay at Waterfall station, the final stop before Cork. The three-car diesel-mechanical unit was introduced to the line in 1954, by which time services had been reduced to two trains a day in each direction. The station sign for Waterfall has been preserved, with other relics, at the nearby Ramble Inn. *D. Lawrence*

Below: A railcar stands beneath the overall roof of Cork Albert Quay station, a relatively small terminus from which passenger services ran to Bandon, Bantry and Baltimore. In spite of its size it had separate First- and Third-class gentlemen's toilets, retaining these until closure. *The Rev J. Parker*

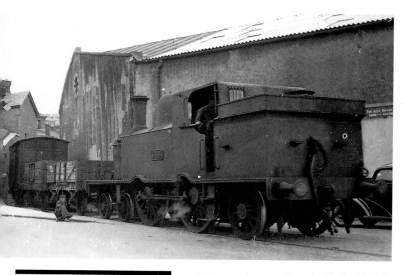

Left: The Cork termini of the CBSCR and GSWR were about a mile apart, and in 1912, to facilitate the transfer of rolling-stock and freight, the Cork City Railways constructed a link which followed Brian Boru Street, one of the city's main thoroughfares. This view, dating from 17 August 1944, features 4-4-2T No 318. The railway trackbed in this area is now a footpath, but little else has changed, and a small section of track remains at Anderson's Quay. *O. Prosser*

Right: Ex-GSWR No 20l, an Ivatt-designed 0-6-0T, heads a train for Albert Quay, on the ex-Cork City Railways line, on 8 August 1960. Although all services over the CBSCR line ceased in 1961 the tramway winding through the city streets and over the River Lee would survive until April 1976, a hand bell rung by railway staff warning of a train's approach. *R. Joanes*

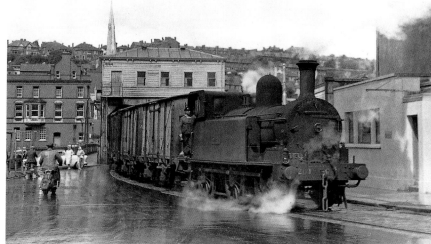

Right: Another view of 4-4-2T No 318, here running onto the bascule bridge on the Cork City Railways on 19 August 1944. Behind can be seen the fine stone exterior of the ex-CBSCR Albert Quay terminus; the gates beside the locomotive's buffer-beam were closed when the river bridge was about to be raised. *O. Prosser*

Left: When the line was closed it was proposed that the Cork City Railways bridges be scrapped, but this provoked uproar, and the bridges were retained for road use. The substantial wooden control boxes above were removed, and the bridges no longer opened to admit river traffic. The main ex-CBSCR station at Albert Quay also survives, as seen here in August 2005, although the trainshed has been demolished. Another survivor is the nearby Albert Street station, which retains its trainshed. *Author*

Left: The first significant closure on the network of lines involved the short-lived branch to Kinsale. This is Ballymartle station, in a 1960s view looking towards Kinsale; the occupants kept the nameboard after closure of the branch by the GSR in 1931. The line had been lifted by 1934, but the trackbed was not formally abandoned until 1962. *J. St Leger*

Below: The view at Farrangalway station, looking towards Kinsale, in the 1960s. The station closed in 1931, but the building remains. *J. St Leger*

Right: The corrugated-iron goods shed at Kinsale remained in May 2005, more than 75 years after closure of the station. The passenger station has been redeveloped for housing, but the platform and iron entrance gateposts remain. The station, high above the picturesque port, was not well placed, while the closure of Kinsale naval base reduced traffic on the branch. *Author*

Centre right: The Bandon included a number of significant engineering works, the greatest of these being Chetwynd Viaduct, over the Owenboy River. This fine structure, 90ft in height and with four 110ft iron spans on stone piers, still survives, being seen here in May 2005. *Author*

Below: Bandon's high-level station buildings, which replaced the low-level station in 1894, survive in use with the local council, as seen here in May 2005. The low-level station became a goods depot and several of its buildings also survive. *Author*

Below right: Closed in 1961, Skibbereen station was the main intermediate station on the Drimoleague–Baltimore line and the interchange point for the narrow-gauge line to Schull. The main-line water tower, goods shed and girder bridge over the River Ilen still survive, and the substantial station goods crane has also been preserved, as seen here in May 2005. *Author*

Ireland became an increasingly popular holiday destination in Victorian times, which prompted the railway companies to build or purchase a number of scenically located hotels. Some were situated in extensive grounds, others constructed in conjunction with golf courses, sea bathing, or fishing. Most were close to railway stations. Combined hotel/railway tickets were also provided to promote tourism.

The MGWR's imposing hotel at Galway, opened in 1852, was the first purpose-built railway hotel in Ireland. The railway later built more remote hotels at Mallaranny and at Recess; a hotel platform was provided at the latter until 1922, when the hotel was burned down during 'The Troubles'.

The GSWR opened hotels at Caragh Lake, Kenmare, Waterville, Parknasilla and Killarney (two). The main hotel at Killarney was built close to the station in 1854, while visitors to the hotel at Parknasilla, set in 180 acres of grounds, were once transported by a horse-drawn coach some 15 miles from Kenmare station. The second hotel built for the GSWR at Killarney, known as the New Hotel, was burned down during 'The Troubles'.

The NCC developed a number of railway hotels. At Portrush the Northern Counties Hotel had more than 100 bedrooms, while the Laharna Hotel at Larne was once the largest tourist hotel in Ireland; both catered for visitors to the Antrim coast and the Giant's Causeway. In Londonderry the NCC also owned the City Hotel. Elsewhere in the North the Slieve Donard Hotel at Newcastle was opened by the BCDR in 1898.

In 1899 the GNR(I) bought hotels at Rostrevor, Warrenpoint and Bundoran, renaming them as Great Northern hotels. The company also took over the hotel at Greenore, which had been opened by the LNWR in 1873.

Not all railway hotels were built specifically for tourism, and many have closed. In Belfast the Midland Hotel was part of York Road station and the first building in Belfast to have electricity; damaged during World War 2, it reopened only to close with the redevelopment of the station. The LNWR ran the North Western Hotel, next to its North Wall station at Dublin; the hotel closed in 1923, but the building remains as railway offices. Another Dublin hotel since converted to office use is the former Station Hotel at Heuston station. At Rathdrum the Station Hotel closed as long ago as 1911, while Limerick Junction Station Hotel closed in 1927, and Cork Station Hotel in 1946.

In 1925 the GSR took over all railway hotels in the Republic, renaming several of the more impressive as Great Southern hotels and building a new one at Sligo. The ex-GNR(I) hotels, like the railway itself, were eventually divided up with the partition of Ireland, but that at Bundoran, after a spell under GSR ownership, has reverted to its Great Northern title. In 1945 the GSR hotels became part of CIE, which eventually sold them; some, including that at Caragh Lake, were subsequently demolished, but most remain in use.

The UTA took over all the railway-owned hotels in Northern Ireland in 1948, and they were sold out of railway ownership in 1966. Unfortunately, once 'The Troubles' took hold in the North only one, the Slieve Donard, survived in use as a hotel, and some, such as the Great Northern Hotel at Rostrevor, were demolished.

Above: The MGWR crest on a fireplace at the Great Southern Hotel at Galway. This 100-bedroom hotel was designed, along with the adjoining station, by J. S. Mulvany. Originally known as the Railway Hotel, it opened in 1852 and was the first purpose-built railway hotel in Ireland. Among its more famous guests were Alcock and Brown, who were welcomed here in 1919 after their epic transatlantic flight. The hotel was renamed as a Great Southern Hotel in 1925 and remains open today. *Author*

Above right: The main entrance to the Great Southern Hotel at Killarney. Designed by Fredrick Darley in a neo-Georgian style, the hotel opened in 1854, located within 100 yards of the station, to which it was originally linked by a covered walkway. Considered by many as the first 'Grand Railway Hotel' in Ireland, it survived 'The Troubles' and remains open to this day. *Author*

There has been much change, but a good selection of one-time railway hotels remain open, and some retain their well-known railway names, notably the Slieve Donard Hotel at Newcastle, the Great Northern Hotel at Bundoran and the Great Southern hotels at Galway, Parknasilla, and Killarney. While only two of these can still be reached directly by train, all now offer, in addition to fabulous locations and hospitality, the opportunity to savour their historic Irish railway past.

Right: Slieve Donard Hotel was served by a siding from Newcastle station, enabling coal to be delivered to the hotel's electricity plant, which also illuminated the station. Construction of the hotel took two years, and it opened in June 1898. The BCDR crest can still be found over the main entrance and is seen here in August 2003. Each of the original 120 bedrooms once had its own fireplace, while sea-water baths were popular. Suitably modernised, the hotel remains open, as does the adjoining golf course. *Author*

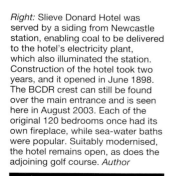

Left: The Great Northern Hotel at Bundoran was owned from 1895 by the GNR(I). Located close to the southern sandy shore of Donegal Bay, it enjoyed fine views over the Donegal hills. It boasted of having electricity and acted as a real fillip for the holiday resort. Both hotel and golf course remain open. *courtesy of The Irish Historical Picture Company*

Left: The CDRJC had considered providing a hotel in 'The Donegal Highlands', but 'The Troubles' put an end to such ideas. The LLSR also encouraged tourism, and clearly also provided unofficial camping sites, as apparent from this scene near Buncrana, recorded on 17 September 1948 from atop the home signal. Road widening — in 1963, after the closure of the railway — has since obscured this view. *I. Wright*

25 The Emerald Isle

There remains great interest in Irish railways and their history. Societies have been established, notably the Railway Preservation Society of Ireland, which has specialised in working steam locomotives, and the Irish Traction Group, which has preserved a wide range of diesels. A score of other railway societies and preservation schemes has also been established, and all help maintain the diverse, delightful and captivating railway history of Ireland. Museums, in particular Cultra, provide a fascinating array of historic engines, stock and memorabilia.

The Downpatrick Railway Museum has preserved a section of the erstwhile BCDR, while the narrow-gauge Waterford & Suir Valley Railway has been established on a section of the trackbed of the old Waterford–Mallow line. Various closed narrow-gauge lines have also had sections preserved, enabling the forgotten delights of Ireland's 'narra'-gauge lines to be relived. The County Donegal, Cavan & Leitrim, Tralee & Dingle and West Clare lines all have preserved sections on which to travel, while sections of the Listowel & Ballybunion Railway — one of the great railway curiosities of the British Isles — and the Giant's Causeway Tramway have reopened.

Although all the original narrow-gauge passenger lines have closed, narrow-gauge turf lines provide the largest single group of industrial railways in Europe. Many are operated by the Bord na Móna, and all transport peat. At Blackwater a summer tourist train is operated on one of the peat-bog lines.

In the North the Knockmore–Antrim line was closed in June 2003. A review of the railways in Northern Ireland considered a series of options, including closure of the Ballymena–Londonderry and the Whiteabbey–Larne lines, but lobbying for the retention of the network was intense, and these lines remain open.

In the Republic a strategic rail review generally backed retention of the existing passenger system. In 2004 the reopening of the Cork–Middleton section of the Youghal branch line was announced. Additionally the Sligo–Claremorris–Athenry–Ennis line was being studied for a possible reopening, as part of the Western Rail Corridor, and work has been authorised for the Athenry–Ennis section. Other closed lines are also being retained for potential future freight use.

Much of historical railway interest remains. Many Victorian railway buildings have been saved, steam sheds converted to diesel depots, and other redundant railway buildings put to various new uses, while disused signalboxes and other railway relics abound.

A modern network of operational lines still unites much of Ireland, many ex-railway hotels continue in use, there is an enormous wealth of fascinating railway heritage, there is beautiful scenery and friendliness to strangers ... all are ingredients for the ideal Irish railway adventure. Irish eyes are smiling.

Right: Adjacent to the ex-BCDR station at Cultra a beautifully restored and representative sample of items from Irish standard- and narrow-gauge railways has been collected at the Ulster Folk & Transport Museum. GSR 4-6-0 No 800 *Maeve* dating from 1939 is seen here looming behind a Great Victoria Street station seat — one of the collection's numerous artefacts from Irish railways. *Author's collection*

Left: A GNR(I) branch provided a connection with CLR trains at Belturbet. Trains last used the station in 1959, after which it became derelict and lost its roof. However, the Belturbet community came together and helped restore the building, which was the only stone-built station designed by William Mills. Other buildings, including the goods store, water tower and engine shed, also survive as seen here in May 2003. The CLR also has a preserved Dromod–Mohill section. *Author*

Right: The ex-BCDR station at Downpatrick closed on 15 January 1950, and although a great loss to this county town is now home to the Downpatrick Railway Museum, which operates a 4-mile section of the old BCDR line. This signalbox, which came from Ballyclare Junction on the NCC, is just one of the many historic items now to be found here, as this new taken in May 2003 shows. *Author*

Left: At Carlingford part of the Newry–Greenore line has been turned into a road, while the stone-built station, closed in 1952, is now used as a tourist information centre. Details of the station's original chimney pots, perhaps designed to reflect the nearby Carlingford Castle, are seen here in May 2003. *Author*

Right: Opened in 1887, the narrow-gauge Clogher Valley Railway ran some 37 miles from Tynan to Maguiresbridge. Trains connected with the GNR(I) at both ends of the line, but with losses mounting it closed to all traffic in December 1941. Mainly a roadside line, it included a number of substantially built stations, including this one in the heart of Augher, seen here in March 2005 in use as a café. *S. Winson*

Right: The Giant's Causeway Tramway was from 1883 powered hydro-electrically by turbines on the River Bush. Closed in 1949, a section reopened in 2002, using much equipment from the Shane Castle Railway, which itself had closed in 1995. *Tyrone*, a Peckett 0-4-0T dating from 1904 (and originally from British Aluminium Works at Larne), is seen in August 2005, with the superbly reproduced traditional station buildings at Giant's Causeway in the background. *P. Stamper*

Left: The County Donegal Railway Heritage Centre is based at Donegal station, which acts as a museum for the railway. *Drumboe*, the impressive 'Baltic' tank, is seen here in its handsome geranium-red livery in August 2005, prior to being overhauled. Part of the ex-CDRJC line along the shores of Lough Finn at Fintown has also been preserved, while further stock is to be found at the Foyle Valley Railway Museum in Londonderry. *P. Stamper*

Left: The Listowel & Ballybunion Railway has seen a remarkable revival, and this curious railway has to be seen to be believed. The world's first working passenger monorail closed in 1924, but a replica of one of the original three Hunslet locomotives, No 4, is seen here at Listowel in May 2005. Together with turntables, track and coaches, it authentically recreates an opportunity to test the riding qualities of this unique line. *Author*

Below left: The Tralee & Dingle Railway, famous for its steep gradients and beautiful scenery, has a preserved section at Tralee. Here also can be found one of the original TDR narrow-gauge locomotives, 2-6-2T No 5T, dating from 1892. The Slieve Mish Mountains can be seen in the background in this view from a train in August 2005. *Author*

Above right: Moyasta Junction was where the West Clare Railway divided for Kilkee and Kilrush. Close to the Atlantic coast and still a remote and wild location, it is now the centre for a revival of the line, and 2-6-2T *Slieve Callan* and other rolling-stock will use the reinstated narrow-gauge section towards Kilkee and Doonbeg. The station sign is seen here in May 2005. *Author*

Right: Much of railway interest survives in Ireland, including lower-quadrant semaphore signals on several of the lines that remain open. An example is to be found at Loo Bridge, on the Kenmare branch, which closed in January 1960; it was photographed in May 2005. *Author*

Far right: Cobh, once known as Queenstown, and where a deep-water quay adjoined the railway station, remains connected to Ireland's national rail network. This view, recorded in August 2005, shows part of the original station, which has been turned into a museum. This traces the harrowing journeys of Irish emigrants who used this station on their journey to North America, including those unfortunate enough to catch the ill-fated *Titanic*, which made its final call here. *Author*

The rugged coastal landscape at Bray Head is enhanced by preserved ex-GSWR 'J15' 0-6-0 No 186, dating from 1879, working an RPSI tour to Wicklow in May 1968 (and still going strong today). Visible on the right is the course of I. K. Brunel's original coastal line, replaced by a more inland tunnel route in 1917 because of erosion. This is just one of the many Irish lines, steeped in history, that are not lost; a friendly and fascinating railway network still remains, awaiting your visit. *A. Donaldson*